POST-INDUSTRIAL URBAN GREENSPACE ECOLOGY, AESTHETICS AND JUSTICE

This book offers original theoretical and empirical insight into the social, cultural and ecological politics of rapidly changing urban spaces such as old factories, rail yards, verges, dumps and quarries. These environments are often disregarded once their industrial functions wane, a trend that cities are experiencing through the advance of late capitalism.

From a sustainability perspective, there are important lessons to learn about the potential prospects and perils of these disused sites. The combination of shelter, standing water and infrequent human visitation renders such spaces ecologically vibrant, despite residual toxicity and other environmentally undesirable conditions. They are also spaces of social refuge. Three case studies in Milwaukee, Paris and Toronto anchor the book, each of which offers unique analytical insight into the forms, functions and experiences of post-industrial urban greenspaces. Through this research, this book challenges the dominant instinct in Western urban planning to "rediscover" and redevelop these spaces for economic growth rather than ecological resilience and social justice.

This book will be of great interest to students and researchers of urban planning, ecological design, landscape architecture, urban geography, environmental planning, restoration ecology and aesthetics.

Jennifer Foster is Associate Professor in the Faculty of Environmental and Urban Change at York University, Canada.

Routledge Equity, Justice and the Sustainable City

Series editors: Julian Agyeman and Stephen Zavestoski

This series positions equity and justice as central elements of the transition toward sustainable cities. The series introduces critical perspectives and new approaches to the practice and theory of urban planning and policy that ask how the world's cities can become 'greener' while becoming more fair, equitable and just.

The *Routledge Equity Justice and the Sustainable City* series addresses sustainable city trends in the global North and South and investigates them for their potential to ensure a transition to urban sustainability that is equitable and just for all. These trends include municipal climate action plans; resource scarcity as tipping points into a vortex of urban dysfunction; inclusive urbanization; "complete streets" as a tool for realizing more "livable cities"; the use of information and analytics toward the creation of "smart cities".

The series welcomes submissions for high-level cutting-edge research books that push thinking about sustainability, cities, justice and equity in new directions by challenging current conceptualizations and developing new ones. The series offers theoretical, methodological, and empirical advances that can be used by professionals and as supplementary reading in courses in urban geography, urban sociology, urban policy, environment and sustainability, development studies, planning, and a wide range of academic disciplines.

Post-Industrial Urban Greenspace Ecology, Aesthetics and Justice
Jennifer Foster

Mapping Possibility
Finding Purpose and Hope in Community Planning
Leonie Sandercock

For more information about this series, please visit: www.routledge.com/ Routledge-Equity-Justice-and-the-Sustainable-City-series/book-series/EJSC

POST-INDUSTRIAL URBAN GREENSPACE ECOLOGY, AESTHETICS AND JUSTICE

Jennifer Foster

Routledge
Taylor & Francis Group
LONDON AND NEW YORK

earthscan
from Routledge

Designed cover image: Jennifer Foster

First published 2023
by Routledge
4 Park Square, Milton Park, Abingdon, Oxon OX14 4RN

and by Routledge
605 Third Avenue, New York, NY 10158

Routledge is an imprint of the Taylor & Francis Group, an informa business

British Library Cataloguing-in-Publication Data
A catalogue record for this book is available from the British Library

ISBN: 978-1-138-09383-6 (hbk)
ISBN: 978-1-032-41077-7 (pbk)
ISBN: 978-1-315-10640-3 (ebk)

DOI: 10.4324/9781315106403

Typeset in Bembo
by Apex CoVantage, LLC

Dedication
For anyone who has worked through a brain injury, in any job whatsoever.

CONTENTS

TERRITORIAL ACKNOWLEDGEMENT

This manuscript was prepared on the traditional territories of numerous Indigenous peoples who took care of the land for thousands of years and continue to do so. The majority of this book was authored on the traditional territories of the Wendake-Nionwentsïo, Mississauga, Mississaugas of the Credit First Nation, Anishinabewaki and Haudenosaunee people. Known as Tkaronto (where trees stand in the water) in the Mohawk language, Toronto is the present-day homeland of diverse First Nations, Inuit and Métis communities. The Algonquian word millioke (beautiful land) and the Potawatomi word minwaking (gathering place by the water) are the basis for the name Milwaukee, where much writing was completed. These are the traditional territories of the Menominee, Bodwéwadmi (Potawatomi), Peoria, Kiikaapoi (Kickapoo) and Myaamia peoples. The traditional territories of the Omàmiwininiwag Algonquin and Anishinabewaki peoples in the Ottawa Valley also hosted much of this writing, and parts of this manuscript were prepared on the traditional territories of the Coast Salish, Stz'uminus, Stó:lō, Musqueam, Squamish and Tsleil-Waytuth.

As a result of historic and current colonialism, Indigenous communities have experienced vast dispossession, anguish and genocide, as well as attempted destruction of their cultures, relationships and spirituality. It is the duty of non-Indigenous people to support Indigenous sovereignty and wellbeing and to continuously learn and practice respectful relationships. Acknowledging the territories of Indigenous People across Turtle Island is a modest but essential act of recognition, which must be joined with commitments to honour and support Indigenous People and their self-determination.

ILLUSTRATIONS

Figures

Tables

PREFACE

The inspiration for this research came from admiration for the ecological systems thriving in old industrial lands. I have lost hundreds of hours in the places described here, fascinated by the inlay of nature throughout industrial ruins. I have been enthralled by the interweaving of unexpected species, the unique ways that animals make use of marginal terrain and the astonishing ability for life to succeed in conditions commonly perceived as spoiled. But these spaces aren't just interesting ecosystems. They are also urban archives, the remains of obsolete industries and testaments to countless people's lives. They trace to neighbourhoods beyond the site borders as well, to community livelihoods. But perhaps most appealingly, they are typically quiet places where one might find a measure of solitude, slow down and become absorbed in the surroundings. They are excellent places to disappear in plain view without leaving the city.

The case studies derive from over a decade and a half of field research in Milwaukee, Paris and Toronto. From a methodological perspective, the research blends analysis of policy and planning documents, archival materials, media products, reports, films and documentaries. These are combined with field research and dozens of interviews. Many of the interviews were conducted on foot or resting among industrial relics, over repeat visits. Many visits were team explorations, not part of formal interviews but laden with insights from knowledgeable and experienced locals. And even more were solo visits, often without a set path, typically extending far beyond anticipated timelines and always generating more questions than answers.

This book focuses on three post-industrial spaces with which I have a personal connection. I spent much of my youth on the edges of Paris, hanging out along rail verges and entering dark tunnels with friends. My introduction to the Petite Ceinture, in the late 1980s, began by crawling through a fence opening at dusk and ended in the morning hours on the opposite side of the city. I was hooked.

Milwaukee is my mother's hometown, where many generations of my family have worked in the factories along the Menomonee Valley. I recall the Valley's industrial vigour, its decline and then its progression into a no-go zone. My uncle's enthusiastic announcement that the Valley was going to be revitalized as a greenspace with a new industry was certainly intriguing. This was, after all, the "armpit of the city," in the Rust Belt during an economic recession. On my next visit to Milwaukee, he brought me into the Valley to see for myself. I was amazed by the vision and mettle. Toronto is where I now live and work, my home base since the mid-1990s. It took a while before I learned to enjoy this city, until the late Michael Hough introduced me to the Leslie Street Spit. I have loved watching the Spit evolve through the past 20+ years. Waiting patiently for newly dumped rubble to eventually transition into verdant habitat has been a great reward in life. I have met some of the most interesting people on the Spit, often with minimal social interaction, and have never had a bad day there. It is one of my favourite places in the world.

As compelling as they are for their biophysical splendour, the evolution of these urban post-industrial greenspaces cannot be considered outside of environmental justice concerns. These spaces beg questions about whose histories are told, in what ways and to what ends. How are communities affected by industrial legacies, in the present? Whose interests are served by efforts to improve these spaces, and how can the communities most affected by de-industrialization ensure that their priorities are articulated and enacted? How do greenspaces sometimes mask injustices? And how can conventional Western aesthetic expectations for greenspaces transition into versions of nature that are responsive to alternative interpretations of ecological health and vibrancy? As I got to know each of these places, they revealed more and more about the complex ways that politics are always embedded in greenspace, especially in post-industrial ones.

ACKNOWLEDGEMENTS

I am deeply grateful to everyone who participated in this research. Dozens of people agreed to be interviewed over the years, sometimes repeatedly so, sometimes in perilous environmental conditions. The insights that they shared with me, many of which are conveyed in quotations throughout this book, are invaluable. I am equally indebted to everyone who ventured as a companion in field explorations, especially when we knew that conditions would be irregular and perhaps perilous. I enjoyed getting lost with each and every one of you, even when we didn't like what we found.

I extend a special thanks to Ilan Kapoor for encouraging me to submit a prospectus with the false premise that it would simply involve converting my published work into book chapters. Thank you for planting the seeds and making this seem viable! Thank you, Luisa Sotomayor, for always injecting enthusiasm into this project, even amid turmoil. Thank you to all my faculty colleagues at York University. Your work and collaboration never cease to inspire me. Andil Gosine, Anna Zalik, Cate Sandilands, Abidin Kusno, Stefan Kipfer, Gail Fraser, Sheila Colla, Liette Gilbert, Anders Sandberg, Honor Ford-Smith, Justin Podur, Lisa Myers and everyone else in the Faculty of Environmental and Urban Change, thank you for creating such a rich scholarly home.

Thank you to the team of students who contributed to this project, particularly Héloïse Hayet, Kumail Raza and Yvonne Masso. The Faculty of Urban and Environmental Change attracts so many talented students, and I am grateful to have continued collaborations with many. I am particularly grateful for ongoing partnerships with Heidy Schopf, Shannon Holness and Jennifer Smith. I always look forward to our next chapters.

I am thankful to the Routledge Equity, Justice and the Sustainable City Series team and appreciate the patience in weathering impediments and hindrances that slowed the completion of this manuscript. In particular, I appreciate the steady support of Stephen Zavestoski and Julian Agyeman, as well as Rosie Anderson, Julia Pollacco, Oindrilla Bose, Matthew Shobbrook and Grace Harrison.

This research was supported by a variety of research grants beginning in 2007. These include three grants from the Canadian Social Sciences and Humanities Research Council (SSHRC) and two small research grants from York University.

Finally, thank you to friends and family. You are blessings in life.

1

INTRODUCTION

This book probes the varied ways that the interpretation of old industrial sites plays into interpretations of nature, how alternative spaces are discerned and what is possible in the future. Industrial disinvestment has deeply transformed cities over the past 50 years, with profound social and ecological consequences. Spatial functions, processes and meanings have all metamorphosed, creating post-industrial conditions in the Global North that are simultaneously predictable, novel and indeterminate. Although the reasons for deindustrialization vary and are sometimes nuanced, in general, there are two major threads that unravel industrial production and ancillary infrastructure: relocation and obsolescence. These may be distinct phenomena, but they intertwine and reify one another through political commitments to neoliberal urbanism. Entire workforces have been exported as corporations shift away from areas with well-paid and unionized labour forces towards locations where wages are low and worker rights are less robust. This is enhanced by free trade agreements, more lenient environmental obligations, amplified automation and increasingly cheaper, easier and more reliable transportation of materials and goods. The economic rationale of deindustrialization is clear, but as High and Lewis (2007) assert, it is not simply an economic process but also a cultural process. It is also a profoundly ecological process.

As communities left in the wake of deindustrialization grapple with the imprint of collapsed livelihoods, these spaces are often regarded as landscape indicators of socio-economic deterioration and ruin. Communities once thriving with quality jobs are frequently left impoverished with the polluted soil, water and air, as well as the physical manifestations of neighbourhood blight. Terrain that was once the locus of production, assembly, livelihood, identity, community relationships and struggle becomes exhausted of its value for capital accumulation. In the pursuit of new means of spinning capital from material and labour extraction, sites left behind often become spaces of mourning and loss.

DOI: 10.4324/9781315106403-1

Amid the neglect and depletion, new spatial relationships emerge through deindustrialization. Sometimes these spaces become green, especially when they are forgotten or left alone. And these are the places where we find some of the most interesting and vibrant urban ecological opportunities. These are always places where the complexities of environmental justice are at play. They are places that invalidate Western aesthetic conventions, opening possibilities for new relationships with nature and alternative ways to engage with the city. They are places that may have the outward appearance of neglect, places that seem disorderly and wild. They may seem disconnected from neoliberal indicators of progress. They may not feel particularly inviting or safe. These spaces are the focus of this book.

This book is not interested in greenspaces that are carefully curated as parks and open spaces designed for human pleasure according to dominant aesthetic sensibilities and interpretations of what is normal and beautiful. Rather, this book explores what is socio-ecologically possible in so-called vacant and abandoned post-industrial remnants. These are special spaces, where unexpected relationships can thrive when productive capacities are suspended, before they are rediscovered in support of capital accumulation. Often depicted as industrial ruins, at times romanticized through visions of otherworldly gothic decay, the aesthetics of post-industrial nature are fascinating. As Edensor (2005) observes,

> While ruins always constitute an allegorical embodiment of a past, while they perform a physical remembering of that which has vanished, they also gesture towards the present and the future as temporal frames which can be read as both dystopian and utopian, and they help to conjure up critiques of present arrangements and potential futures.
>
> *(15)*

This book is concerned with the ways that industrial legacies are rendered ecological. How does nature self-organize when we walk away and leave it alone? Who finds pleasure in these spaces? Who finds refuge? Whose needs are met, and whose are not? What do these spaces tell us about alternative futures, about possibilities unrealized in the urban mainstream? Writing about the former Allied Textiles mill in New Jersey, Cal Flyn (2021) describes "a potent symbol of the decline of American manufacturing, of communities that once depended on it, and the toxic legacies of the industrial era more widely" (138). She rejoins this bleak reality with the following observations about visiting the site in its abandonment, as a contemporary industrial ruin:

> In an urban environment, entering an abandoned space is the nearest thing we have to stepping off the map. It offers anonymity, the succor of green space – without the order, the omnipresence of man, so implicit in the park of garden. An urban ruin might offer an effect upon the mind akin to slipping into a dark forest, or scaling a rugged peak, that same wild element, and we might seek it out for similar reasons. Amid the tumbling mills and

towering, blackened chimneys – the skeletal remains of industrial giants – I feel a flickering, a stirring of the soul; the shadow of the sublime passes overhead.

(145)

Typically characterized as wastelands, these are spaces of ecological virility, even when they are classified as contaminated. In urban settings, it is the absence of management that enables ecological richness. They can teach us a great deal about how nature prospers, especially in comportments that humans might not be accustomed to recognizing. Understanding these as distinct ecosystems, as critical habitat, can only enhance our collective ecological literacy and ability to envision and move towards more sustainable urban futures. This echoes Anna Tsing's (2015) enthusiasm for the unexpected lives and diversity of companion species in heavily damaged and destroyed landscapes and her advocacy for "living in the ruins." Tsing situates humans as part of the disturbance regime and recognizes contemporary time as essentially precarious – vulnerable, unpredictable, unstable and indeterminate. Urging us to "watch unruly edges" and be sensitive to shifting assemblages and the ways that multispecies worlds evolve through unintentional patterns for collaborative survival, Tsing notes that "Blasted landscapes are what we have, and we need to explore their life-promoting patches" (108).

In addition to being potential ecological assets, post-industrial urban greenspaces are home environments, places of social and cultural value that might also be easily overlooked or underestimated. In particular, these spaces often hold deep significance for marginalized communities and neighbourhoods in decline. What appears as urban blight or waste to some may be a space of deep meaning and attachment for others. The histories of old industrial landscapes may be cherished with positive associations like work, livelihood, sustenance, community cohesion and wellbeing. They may also evoke less positive or mixed histories of toil and exhaustion, exploitation and struggle, illness and accidents or of hopes and dreams unrealized. Landscape scars, even when perceived as ugly and uncomfortable indicators of past lives, are often honoured by local communities as emblems of previous times when things were different, before the hardship of industrial decline. They might stir attachments to people and communities whose labour helped shape the landscape, and local communities might not be anxious to dispense with the remaining manifestations of previous times. For local communities, the emotional attachments can encompass complex combinations of feelings like pride and despondence, accomplishment and sorrow, self-esteem and melancholy. They may also remain hopeful about industrial revival that the ruins will be put back into production. Local attitudes about possible futures for these spaces typically fluctuate, with a range of attachments that ebb, flow and evolve.

This book is concerned with post-industrial urban greenspaces that are on the margins, existing outside of the dominant logic of urban development and propriety. The book focuses on urban landscapes of the Global North, where substantial deindustrialization has been ongoing for at least half a century through policies and programs of globalization and global capitalism. It is also where colonialism is rooted and where landscape ideals of colonialism are heavily reproduced against historic ecological relationships. There is no monolithic Global North for which generalizations universally apply, just as the same must be noted with regard to the Global South. Indeed, many of the key themes of this book could also be fruitfully explored in urban centres of the Global South, where the effects of mobile capital and planned obsolescence inevitably produce post-industrial urban sites. This book specifically focuses on areas known as the West, where a large representation of European ethnic groups have stifled alternate socio-ecological relationships. Situated within the context of global capitalism, this book will hopefully contribute to advancing critical dialogue around the imprint of European whiteness as a dominant cultural construct in urban form. Expressed through the ecosystems that are reproduced, the spaces that are valued, the people and communities that are prioritized and the aesthetic conventions that are privileged, nature itself is drafted into the project of European cultural and political control. As messy, indeterminate, leftover landscapes, post-industrial urban greenspaces are fissures in the idealized neoliberal future that is centred on urban policies, plans and designs across the Global North. They offer insight into what is going on and how we might rechannel the momentum of destruction, neglect and inequity to produce more ecologically robust and socio-culturally just cities.

Anna Jorgensen (2012), in the introduction to the edited volume *Urban Wildscapes*, tells us that wildscape is not just a spatial designation but a way of thinking about urban space beyond the "normal commissioning process for the built environment, policing, surveillance and the ways in which places are contextualized within the official cultural narratives of the city" (2). These are places shaped primarily by non-human agency, and they offer some of the most promising potentialities for robust urban ecological systems. They do not correspond with historic reference systems, comprising novel ecosystems in what might be considered *terrain vague*. They are often unwelcoming, ugly, fetid and precarious by conventional park design standards. Yet, they offer important urban amenities: places where movements are less regulated, where socio-cultural norms are loosened, where activities that are inhibited elsewhere in the city are tolerated and where people might fulfil their livelihoods.

A through–line in this book is urban environmental justice, as both an analytical framework for understanding the most important dynamics of post-industrial space and a range of priorities for any type of sustainable urban future. This builds on Anguelovski's (2014) assertion that urban environmental justice is holistic work that is place-based and multifaceted, combining concerns like housing, open space, employment, education, food, health and self-determination. When communities mobilize to reclaim derelict industrial lands in their neighbourhoods and reconstruct them in response to their own needs and ideals, they are also insisting on investment in places and people who are currently there, rather than cultivating new communities with more money and different tastes. This stands in contrast to conventional ways of addressing old industrial land and related infrastructure by declaring them brownfields, decontaminating to a certain standard and then reintroducing them into the capital market as hot urban real estate opportunities.

This book positions aesthetics as a critical interface to the urban landscape experience. The focus is on the everyday aesthetics of local environments, as both cognitive and emotional fields that are meaningful for urban sustainability. Alex Loftus' (2012) proposal for extending praxis into environmental politics accentuates the aesthetic as a key plane for meaning and action, describing the challenge as rooted in the "quotidian relationships" of socio-natural sensual practices. He explains the approach:

> It differs profoundly from the dominant environmental movement in which an environmental vanguard is responsible for instilling new ways of working on an otherwise unthinking populace. If we extend the boundaries of praxis into both the socio-natural realm (it was always there, although not explicitly) *and* extend these experiences into the aesthetic experience, recapturing sensuous experience in the process, then, I argue, we have the possibility for a radical politics from which we might remake our cities in sensuously rich, radically democratic and beautiful ways.
>
> *(126)*

Some of the most spectacular urban ecological transformations of post-industrial spaces are the result of neglect, rather than overt planning and design decisions. A well-known example is the Templehof shunting yard in Berlin, Germany, where ecological succession is stunning and has produced distinctive habitat without human interference. Now known as Natur-Park Südgelände, this former switch-yard and marshalling yard is rich with diverse habitat, thanks to four decades of landlocked existence with the division of Germany following the Second World War. Operations shrunk gradually until it was completely shuttered in 1952, geographically isolated by Cold War politics. Vegetation grew wild and animals made full use of the rapidly evolving habitat during this period of isolation from industrial operations and human usage. Kowarik and Langer (2005) describe how by 1981 natural succession "had led to a richly structured mosaic of dry grasslands, tall herbs, shrub vegetation and individual woodlands." Remarkably, they found that only ten years later, the proportion of woodlands had doubled to 70% of the site and that rare and threatened species had been established in the dry grasslands. By 1995, species richness was astounding, with 366 vascular plants, 208 wild bees and wasps, dozens of breeding birds, 49 macrofungi, 57 spiders and over a dozen grasshoppers and crickets (Kowarik & Langer, 2005).

Unsurprisingly, there were competing land use plans when Germany reunited and quarantined spaces such as the Templehof freight yard became accessible. The site may have been confined, but it was nonetheless frequented by humans during its political isolation. Urban adventurers, wilderness enthusiasts and homeless people all visited (Langer, 2012), many of whom advocated in favour of preserving the unique ecosystems that had evolved on site. Beginning in the 1980s, a group of mobilized residents lobbied for ecological surveys and conservation of the site as urban wilderness, rather than the return of the shunting station. In 1996, ownership was transferred from the rail company to the city, contingent upon its perpetuation as an urban wilderness park. It opened as a park five years later, with 3.2 hectares of nature reserve that is off limits to humans. In its current state, the site maintains a high level of fidelity to both industrial relics and ecological succession, with tracks, pumps, lampposts, a turntable, a stream locomotive and a 50-m-high water tower left intact amid the dry grasslands, herbaceous communities and woodlands. A fresh approach to park planning and design that celebrates the ecological systems springing from urban industrial demise presents what Kowarik and Langer (2005) term "a new wilderness."

In other instances, valued greenspace is established through struggles for what Lefebvre coins the "right to the city," the ability to use and shape the city for one-self, independent of state control, ownership of property or the primacy of capital. These campaigns can be considered through a lens of critical urban planning. They are strategies that are grounded in the experiences and desires of local communities while enhancing knowledge, power and collective action. Often in these cases, the fount of urban greenspace establishment on former urban industrial lands is community resistance to privatization and gentrification, in favour of public access to nature's bounty. This is the case in the Kaka'ako community of Honolulu, where working-class residents mobilized to successfully block a network of expensive residential towers proposed on public lands along the ocean waterfront. The shoreline

FIGURE 1.1 Natur-Park Südgelände, 2012

Source: Image by J. Foster

had traditionally been an environment for recreation and for essential activities like cleansing, fishing, canoe landing, burial and religious practices (Wu, 2007). It transitioned into industrial lands in the mid-1800s with operations like the Honolulu Iron Works that occupied 10 acres and employed over 500 workers (Cole, 2013). The community's blue-collar identity is rooted in the prominent history of salt production, as well as smaller facilities like soy and poi factories, abundant garages, wharfs and shipyards, icehouses and seafood packing, laundries, cleaners and workshops like the Kamaka Ukulele factory. Kelly (2005) characterizes Kaka'ako as the "industrial back alley of Honolulu," and the community sustained a great deal of worker housing. It is also a beloved local surf area, one of the last open shorelines in Honolulu.

Positioned between the intense high-end tourism of Waikiki Beach and the bustle of downtown Honolulu, Kaka'ako is one of the last communities that is accessible for poor and working-class residents. So it wasn't surprising that community members would be upset when the state announced plans for privatization and residential tower development along the Kaka'ako shoreline. It may have been a brownfield, but it was a cherished urban asset that locals were not willing to forsake. The state had taken full control of planning in the broader Kaka'ako neighbourhood in 1976, and overdue improvements to sewage, roads, electricity and other infrastructure were supposed to benefit local residents. But it turned out that these were actually creating the conditions to attract intensive development, to sell the land to condominium developers for exclusive towers. Ron Iwami (2014) captured the community's sentiments at a 2005 rally when he said, "I'm not going to feel welcome and you're not going to feel welcome. It is going to be for the tourists like Waikiki. This is all we got left" (26). A coalition of Kaka'ako community groups formed to resist the planned developments along the shoreline. They organized rallies, attended public input meetings, created a "friends" group and were joined by neighbourhood boards and area legislators, as well as the general public. This turned into a broader public coalition called Save Our Kaka'ako that was not just fighting for the Kaka'ako shoreline, but for all public lands in Hawaii. They distributed t-shirts that became walking billboards throughout the city, organized a People's March to the state capitol, testified at meetings with legislators and in public hearings, met with the state governor and coordinated community celebrations. Eventually, they succeeded in completely blocking the privatization plans and development proposals, in favour of a community-based plan based on fourteen guiding principles that reflect priorities like community cultural gathering, Native Hawaiian values and traditional and customary rights and practices, open view planes and expanded park and green space. As Iwami (2014) explains, all of this was accomplished through community mobilization, without any attorneys or lawsuits. Today, the shoreline is open and accessible, with a long promenade and locals paddling out to join the surf lineup.

This book suggests possibilities of urban post-industrial greenspace that are based on ecological resilience, meaningful public engagement, community-specific priorities and an aesthetic of urban wilderness. The chapters that follow illustrate some of these possibilities in specific urban environments. The profound differences in the trajectories of each case study suggest that there is no formula or set of best practices for planning or designing these spaces. Nor is there a single lens through which to interpret the dynamics at play. They are all sites of job loss, community destruction, environmental injustice and pollution. Until recently, they are all spaces where ecological wellbeing was not a prominent consideration. In each instance, we learn something different about urban environmental justice, novel ecologies, ways of inhabiting newly formed greenspaces, aesthetic possibilities and alternative approaches to planning urban planning and design.

The first chapter sets a conceptual framework for post-industrial urban greenspace, focusing on the interplay between ecological and socio-political systems. The chapter is driven by concern about the ways that ecology can serve as politics by other means, and suggests a constellation of key points around which analytical insight might be generated. Grounded in urban political ecology, the chapter urges deeper investment in the findings of urban ecological sciences, as well as fields like racial capitalism, queer ecologies and anti- and decolonial ecologies. Novel ecosystems are proposed as an apposite interpretation of post-industrial urban greenspace, especially where management regimes are suspended and ecosystems flourish. Environmental justice is always a necessary reading of socio-ecological systems, and this requires an approach that considers not just decontamination of polluted

FIGURE 1.2   Kaka'ako shoreline, 2018

Source: Image by J. Foster

sites, but the histories of such places, how adverse impacts are experienced locally, how coalitions are built and how struggles for sustainable futures are shaped. This ties directly into environmental aesthetics and the right of local residents to shape their own communities according to their own preferences and aesthetic ideals. Aesthetics are approached as multi-sensory experiences that engage whole bodies and evoke emotional responses. They are socially mediated, yet they are mutable and can be adapted to new information and experiences. Aesthetic conceptions of *terrain vague* and *délaissés urbains* – unregulated and indeterminate space on the periphery of the urban mainstream – are explored as opportunities to unfetter ecological and socio-cultural experience from the dominant logic of urbanized capitalism and allow for alternative experiences of nature.

Three case studies are investigated through dedicated chapters. These offer in-depth explorations of the nuanced ways that each site has evolved. Each study explores an expansive, linear portion of a once heavily industrialized urban land-scape, and each tells a different story about the range of possibilities. There is no template for best practices that correspond with the histories, ecosystems and par-ticular community needs of each space.

The case studies begin with the Menomonee Valley, in Milwaukee, USA. Once the "machine shop of the world," this is a part of the American industrial heartland that was hard hit by stagnation and then a dramatic decline in manufacturing. It is a blue-collar city, where heavy industry thrived for centuries, leaving a legacy of extensive pollution. Milwaukee is also known as America's most racially segregated city, with the Menomonee Valley serving as the historic dividing line. Commu-nities living around the edges of the Valley maintain a direct connection to the jobs that it once hosted, so it wasn't surprising that their vision for regeneration prioritized the recovery of family-supporting manufacturing employment. The story of how those jobs were restored is fascinating, and it is rooted in a diverse coalition that foregrounded environmental justice in locally-specific ways, accord-ing to community needs and the social determinants of health. But it is also a story about Indigenous self-determination, and successful environmental justice struggles waged hundreds of kilometres away. The revitalization of Milwaukee's Menomonee Valley from the abandoned and overgrown "armpit of the city" to a network of greenspaces laced with new industry supporting thousands of manu-facturing jobs is remarkable. It is a complex trajectory, with serious challenges and unresolved tensions.

The Petite Ceinture is an ecological windfall for the city of Paris. Imagine the verdant habitat that sprung out of this 32-km continuous, closed rail loop when it was decommissioned in the 1980s and 1990s and left for the wild. It quickly evolved into a fertile *terrain vague*, an oasis of green, a sanctuary tucked amid the city's intensive bustle. Humans also made good use of the space, in diverse ways. As ecological successional stages gave way, the novel ecosystems that formed across the Petite Ceinture comingled with industrial infrastructure and human inhabitations in ways that are otherwise unavailable in the rest of the city. Winding completely around the city, the Petite Ceinture transects socio-economic gradients, passing from Paris' most elite to most marginalized communities in a continuous manner. For some, this self-organizing corridor is a precious urban asset that should be left as is. For others, it is *terra nullius*, awaiting conscription into the land-based cycles of urban capitalism. The planning of this post-industrial greenspace has been more restrained than might be expected if it weren't for the stubborn proprietor: the state rail company. Strategies like temporary urbanism have been taken up to quell discomfort with the line's purported status as an urban void. For the most part, people using the tracks have been left alone, except when specific ethnic groups take over visible segments. It remains largely ambiguous, uneven terrain, where "unplanning" is rationalized as the most desirable short-term future, with distinct environmental justice dynamics and an appreciation for scruffy, unscenic nature.

The Leslie Street Spit, in Toronto, Canada, presents the third case study. This world-class birding locale is also a dump jutting out from the city's industrial lakefront. Like the Menomonee Valley and the Petite Ceinture, it was not planned or designed as habitat; it was simply ignored. While serving as an active dump, this 5-km lakefill developed into a "happy accident," a feral landscape of urban wilderness. Sprouting from the city's building rubble, the ecological communities that evolved on the Spit are also celebrated in narratives about nature's ability to heal itself amid the industrial ruin. This perspective has great appeal, as it lends credence to the idea that nature can eventually compensate for environmental damage, helping to perpetuate cycles of creative destruction. What it does not account for are the communities that are demolished in the name of neoliberal progress, for instance, poor and working-class and Indigenous communities. In these ways, the Spit illustrates how greenspace can assist in historic erasures and mythologize human–nature relationships that are highly politicized. The environmental aesthetics of the Spit also obscure the perilous environmental conditions that wildlife are exposed to as they are drawn to toxic habitat. As a classic *terrain vague*, the Spit is a space of socio-ecological refuge, a low-surveillance, unruly alternative to the urban mainstream. It is rightly celebrated as a spectacular urban ecological asset, and it reveals a great deal about how nature can function as politics by other means.

As often occurs when one is swept away with a topic, conducting research produces more questions. This is certainly the case with this book. Writing this book has felt like an always incomplete endeavour, something that can never be concluded. Communities are constantly changing, ecosystems are in perpetual flux. Urban ecology is a very young field, and each month new studies reveal intriguing insights that enrich our understanding of urban lifeforms. These are unresolved stories about indeterminant spaces. But they disclose a great deal about the complexities of living in cities amidst industrial deterioration. They suggest that there is no universal, predictable pathway through which these spaces become green and that they will evolve in dynamic and surprising ways. They suggest that there are no standardized "best practices" for planning these spaces to yield an ideal future. They suggest that the best strategies may grow from the very communities that are most directly affected by industrial legacies. They suggest that aesthetic expectations can deeply limit urban ecological prospects. And they affirm that ecology is indeed profoundly political.

Bibliography

Anguelovski, I. (2014). *Neighborhood as refuge: Community reconstruction, place remaking, and environmental justice in the city.* The MIT Press.

Cole, W. (2013, September 16). The past lives of Kakaako. *Historic Hawaii Foundation News.* http://historichawaiifoundationnews.blogspot.com/2013/09/the-past-lives-of-kakaako.html.

Edensor, T. (2005). *Industrial ruins: Space, aesthetics and materiality.* Berg.

Flyn, C. (2021). *Islands of abandonment: Nature rebounding in the post-human landscape.* Viking.

High, S., & Lewis, D. W. (2007). Corporate wasteland: The landscape and memory of deindustrialization. *Between the Lines.*

Iwami, R. (2014). *Save our Kaka'ako: A story of the power of the people.* Mutual Publishing.

Jorgensen, A. (2012). Introduction. In A. Jorgensen & R. Keenan (Eds.), *Urban wildscapes* (pp. 1–14). Routledge.

Kelly, J. (2005, May 22). Grit, history of Kakaako shouldn't be wiped clean. *Pacific Business News.* www.bizjournals.com/pacific/stories/2005/05/23/editorial2.html.

Kowarik, I., & Langer, A. (2005). Natur-park Südgelände: Linking conservation and recreation in an abandoned railyard in Berlin. In I. Kowarik & S. Körner (Eds.), *Wild urban woodlands* (pp. 287–299). Springer-Verlag.

Langer, A. (2012). Pure urban nature: Nature-park Südgelände, Berlin. In A Jorgensen & R. Keenan (Eds.), *Urban wildscapes* (pp. 152–159). Routledge.

Loftus, A. (2012). *Everyday environmentalism: Creating and urban political ecology.* University of Minnesota Press.

Tsing, A. L. (2015). *The mushroom at the end of the world: On the possibility of life in capitalist ruins.* Princeton University Press.

Wu, N. (2007, August 3). Kakaako rich with Hawaiian history: Hundreds of Iwi have been uncovered in the area, which once was a thriving community. *Honolulu Star Bulletin.* http://archives.starbulletin.com/2007/08/03/business/story02.html.

2

CONCEPTUALIZING URBAN POST-INDUSTRIAL GREENSPACE

Contemporary patterns of urban de-industrialization are unmistakable across Europe and North America, and the loss has intensified inequities in compound ways that will be felt by generations to come. The roots of de-industrialization are multi-faceted, including factors like the pervasive pressures of automation, urban policies that prioritize service industries, relocation to lower-cost manufacturing centres in the Global South, innovations in cargo transport and the demand for ever more expansive production sites. Deindustrialization has triggered what Gobster (2012) calls a "cascade of abandonment" across urban lands that produce highly disturbed and contaminated open space. Neighbourhoods that once thrived as industrial centres now find themselves in transition. Sometimes, these newly formed open spaces are reinvented according to the edicts of the new economy, for instance, as sprawling warehouse distribution centres or high-density mixed-use condominium developments. Sometimes, they become redesigned as extraordinary public parks or civic facilities. But other times, they are simply left alone, deserted as superfluous infrastructure that is not worth saving.

There are stunning examples of carefully designed urban greenspaces constructed on former industrial sites. Chicago's Millennium Park, Atlanta's BeltLine, Paris' Coulée Verte, Crescent Park in New Orleans, London's Queen Elizabeth Olympic Park and Seattle's Gas Works Park are but a sample of the many urban spaces that have been completely reconfigured for public use. These are spaces that were decontaminated (or at least rendered consistent with local regulations governing the desired after-use of the space), resurfaced and replanted to create welcoming, open access for leisuring crowds. They are newly inserted parks, inaccessible only a few decades ago but now convivial places to gather and recreate. However, as impressive as these projects may be, they are often ecologically hostile environments. They are places where wildlife is unwelcome and uninvited plants are weeded out. They are also places that are heavily socially controlled, where codes

DOI: 10.4324/9781315106403-2

of behaviours are strictly prescribed and monitored. In contrast to these striking parks, abandoned or neglected industrial spaces, pestilent and unsightly as they may be by conventional Western standards, tend to produce some of the most ecologically rich and socially unconstrained greenspaces.

How can we build an understanding of post-industrial urban greenspace that is mindful of the interplay between biophysical, social and cultural dynamics? This chapter considers a variety of perspectives that work in concert to build dialogue between these currents in service of wild urban nature. Bringing science into urban analysis and urban analysis into science is a first step. Doing so entails the interpretation of these spaces within processes of urbanized capitalism while resisting their classification as ecologically degraded. Their existence as novel ecologies distinguishes them from received wisdom about what is natural and how ecosystems function. As core grounds for struggles against environmental injustices in urban landscapes, post-industrial greenspaces are crucial to any critical interpretations of how nature evolves politically. Evaluating the Anthropocene as more of a boundary event than an epoch, Donna Haraway (2016) encourages rejection of bitter cynicism, faith in technofixes or a "game over" attitude. Rather, it is through unexpected collaborations and combinations that we are able to respond to devastating events, cultivate refuges and "become-with others for a habitable, flourishing world" (168). In post-industrial urban greenspace, environmental aesthetics are the primary interface through which the socio-politics of nature are experienced, and they offer a strategic juncture for Haraway's call to "stay with the trouble." In this spirit, the concepts of *terrains vague* and *délaissés urbains* are conceptualizations of urban nature that have the capacity to disrupt the dominant logic of capitalism and open remarkably generative ecological and social possibilities.

Urban politics, urban ecosystems

The biophysical dimensions of urban ecosystems are largely overlooked and poorly understood. While scientific knowledge about ecology is entirely relevant to urban settings, since ecological systems are omnipresent and inescapable, there is a persistent Western cultural assumption that "real" ecosystems have been displaced from cities and what remains is artifice recombined through successive waves of structural transformation to the point where supposed natural attributes no longer exist. This misunderstanding that cities are devoid of nature, not ecologically interesting, or environmentally degraded also pervades the physical and natural sciences. As Niemala (2000) succinctly explains, "Traditionally, ecologists have been reluctant to study urban ecosystems, because they have been regarded as inferior to less disturbed rural areas" (57). According to this logic, cities are places where nature has been demolished, and ecological attention is properly focused on less sullied environs that are not so heavily affected by human activity. This is the legacy of prominent ecological narratives that imagine nature as pristine and organic, uncorrupted by urbanization. And it is a narrative that is, thankfully, being remit as a disingenuous interpretation of both science and cities.

Writing in the mainstream *New York* magazine in 2010, Robert Sullivan notes the interruption of popular conceptions of urban ecology and a nascent shift in scientific perspective. He observes that "The way we currently think about nature in New York is that nature, for the most part, has skipped town." But he also points to a burgeoning awareness among scientists that "It is no longer strange to hear ecologists talk about urban wilderness." Still, for the most part, biological and physical sciences generally remain uninterested in urban areas, an obstinate habit of thinking that is reflected in the journals, academic curricula and funding priorities that dominate the disciplinary approaches. At the other end of the spectrum, there is also a scarcity of serious attention to ecological matters in urban-focused social sciences and humanities. When ecological systems are acknowledged within these fields, the treatment is typically superficial, glossed over as though nature is a category that either speaks for itself or does not warrant careful consideration. Urban ecology is commonly perceived as both distinct from and less important to urban composition than concerns such as housing, transit, capital development, equity or governance. When the concept of ecology does appear in the social sciences and humanities, it is frequently employed in a metaphoric sense, in the extreme abstract, as simple wordplay, or left stranded without much more than the suggestion that there is far more going on. This is even true in fields like urban studies, sociology and political science that are attuned to the spatial formations and physical settings within which socio-political dynamics are enacted, where even the most simplistic acknowledgement of ecological systems is often greeted as revelatory yet unworthy of serious analysis of the material and biophysical implications of non-human lifecycles in cities.

Thankfully, clusters of research and thought dedicated to understanding urban ecology are incubating and discernible in diverse scholarly approaches. For instance, the catalogues of research pertaining to urban wildlife, climate, hydrology and air quality are becoming increasingly robust. Much of this work focuses on understanding ecosystem services as benefits to humans living in dense settlements. These research agendas investigate ways that nature can provide the means to do desirable things like filter dirty air, relieve urban heat island effects, mitigate disasters, assist pollination and food production or moderate the release of industrial effluents. Nature is simultaneously envisioned as a set of instruments and a strategy for enhancing the livelihoods and experiences of humans. These studies employ scientific methods to develop vital insights into the biophysical forces that form the undercurrents of urban life, for the benefit of humans, to both attenuate potential damage and restore the scars of historic ecological degradation. However, there is still some degree of incoherence across different studies. In an effort to enhance the quality of policy and planning decisions, MacGregor-Fors (2011) seeks to establish common terminology across urban ecological studies, noting that "synonyms of basic urban ecology terms have been used by researchers to describe different environmental conditions, while similar conditions are often described using diverse terms" (347). Despite this lack of coherence and an overtly instrumentalist appreciation of ecosystems, these clusters of research set out the essential baseline knowledge for any environmentally cognizant urban policy or planning, especially as the demands for a more sustainable future gain popularity. Meanwhile, work emerging from fields like environmental ethics, cultural environmental studies and landscape architecture offers inroads into understanding the complex non-utilitarian relationships between nature and humans in urban settings. And fields like human ecology, landscape ecology and cultural geography have cultivated advanced research and focused conversations about nature and cities.

How can we develop an understanding of the complex ways that ecological systems can function as politics by other means? The conjoined analytical perspectives of critical political ecology and urban political ecology offer nuanced insights, particularly in terms of understanding how greenspaces exist as products of capitalism combined with racism and other forms of oppression. Probing biophysical transformations through the lens of urbanization as a process of capital accumulation helps interpret cities as socio-natural assemblages that are alive and constantly in flux. Neil Smith's (1984) rebuff of the notion of a pure or pristine version of nature provides the analytical foundation, arguing that nature is produced through everyday struggles of capitalist relationships that include distribution, exchange and consumption. He traces how the "fate" of nature is determined by demands of capitalist production that are fuelled by the desire for ever-expanding profit (in the form of exchange value, rather than the fulfilment of basic needs) that produces a "second nature" that is internalized within the capitalist economic system. As incisive an insights as this is, some argue that Smith's approach is anthropomorphic in that it does not adequately appreciate non-human agency as fundamental to socio-natural assemblage [for instance, Whatmore (2002) and Castree (2000)]. David Harvey (1996) builds on Smith's work with the insistence that nature-capital relations are heterogeneous, meaning that they are temporally and locationally specific, allowing for a less deterministic interpretation that is open to potential positive and negative socio-ecological experiences of similar phenomena. By challenging neoliberal market logic and advocating for urban transformations in the context of Henri Lefebvre's (1968) "right to the city," Harvey champions the collective power to direct the processes of urbanization, and in doing to exert control over and shape the qualities of human life. Harvey (2008) explains:

> The question of what kind of city we want cannot be divorced from that of what kind of social ties, relationship to nature, lifestyles, technologies and aesthetic values we desire. The right to the city is far more than the individual liberty to access urban resources: it is a right to change ourselves by changing the city.

This is an interpretation of urbanization that is not so much fixated on current form and functions but rather is invested in who has the ability to shape cities and what is possible going forward. Contemporary visions of the right to the city are often less radical than Lefebvre's, adopting liberal-democratic inclinations that sometimes work within the state apparatus (Purcell, 2013). For example, participatory planning models that advance the capacities of local residents, particularly those who are marginalized, are important instruments that may be employed. Right to the city strategies tend to be long term, and they are mobilized in diverse spheres through multi-dimensional intervention approaches. Planning and design approaches in this spirit supersede institutional structures, along the lines of Jeremy Till's (2005) transformative participation built through what he terms the "expert citizen/citizen expert," which goes beyond normative practices of "soothing gestures" or "manipulation through the false guise of inclusion." A right to the city lens extends into all realms of urban interaction that aim to resist displacement, reclaim control over neighbourhoods and enable residents to determine the future of these spaces. Strategies prioritize the voices and needs of poor and working-class residents as well as Black, Latino and other marginalized populations. These approaches tend to be unconcerned with citizenship and focus instead on inhabitation. Initiatives can range from campaigns for eviction bans, labour rights, accessible education, food justice, culturally responsive infrastructure and services, aesthetic justice or health equity. Right to the city can also include more clandestine, self-determined interventions, for instance, decisions to inhabit underutilized buildings and greenspaces, cultivate gardens in vacant lots or create artistic expressions on public walls.

Urban political ecology is an effective point of departure for interpreting the inlay of capitalism into contemporary forms of nature in cities. By insisting on processes of urbanization, rather than static urban forms, as the appropriate analytical mode, urban political ecology presents a line of investigation that is particularly fitting in the milieus of post-industrial spaces. The compositions of cities are constantly changing, communities are transformed both exogenously and from within and ecosystems are continually evolving. Infusing these dynamics are the forces of capital accretion and transfiguration that cycle through the extraction of materials and labour, production and surplus, market saturation, disinvestment and waste, propelling the existence of post-industrial urban space. This process is equally at play among sites that are re-purposed into the real estate market and those that are abandoned. The greenspaces that emerge in the post-industrial wake have evolved ecologically as a result of capitalism, as have the relationships of these greenspaces within the wider surrounding landscapes. Materials accumulated through the legacies of industrial production (such as heavy metals, built infrastructure and workers' tools) intermingle with materials that predate production (such as mineral substrates, groundwater reservoirs and seedbanks) to form habitat that attracts new species and the food webs that form around them. Meanwhile, these spaces become capital surplus once they are unprofitable in the economic market, in spite of any meaning or role they may have once occupied in people's lives.

Urban political ecology is particularly illuminating in the conceptualization of the politically determined fluxes of energy and materials through cities as urban metabolism (Heynen et al., 2006). This helps clarify the paired transformations of biophysical and socio-cultural phenomena as a ceaseless process that is fundamental to urban life. For instance, there are rich conversations traced through the flows of water [such as Swyngedouw et al. (2002) and Kaika (2012)], as illustrated by Gandy (2004):

> Water is not simply a material element in the production of cities but is also a critical dimension to the social production of space. Water implies a series of connectivities between the body and the city, between social and bio-physical systems, between the evolution of water networks and capital flows, and between the visible and invisible dimensions to urban space. But water is at the same time a brutal delineator of social power which has at various times worked to either foster greater urban cohesion or generate new forms of political conflict.
>
> *(373)*

More recent developments in urban political ecology have shifted the analytical lens towards interpretations of power that centre cultural politics and are more aligned with critical political ecology's concern with changing power relations of intersecting actors at different scales. Drawing on Foucault's (1973, 1978) interpretation of power formed through discourse as social practice, critical political ecology contextualizes capitalism with knowledge production as constitutive of power dynamics that discipline individual bodies, communities, organizations, political systems, global relations and what is possible in the world. This is a promising evolution of the field for those concerned with the tenacity of matters such as white supremacy, the police state, carceral ethos, heteronormative urbanities, and the lasting imprint of colonial legacies on cities. Further, it is generative in terms of moving beyond material dispossession to also consider non-material concerns, for instance, the interplay between ecological decision-making and representational sovereignty. As urban political ecology is awakening to the intersectional oppressions of contemporary socio-natures, the field is also diffusing into broader conversations about what constitutes equity, what the political and ethical allegiances of researchers might look like and what types of futures are both desirable and possible. The gates of the field have been thrown wide open, such that theoretical perspectives no longer hang upon close readings of Marx but rather are rooted in diverse theoretical frameworks with a broader range of anti-oppression commitments.

Research and thought tackling racial capitalism offer insights into the currents that charge compound oppressions, and this is a direction that urban political ecology is increasingly turning in its reconnaissance of uneven development. Focusing on capitalism as a device and system for manipulating and exploiting Black and Brown communities (and racial exploitation as an imperative of capitalism), this constellation of work also elucidates how nature is racialized through economic inequities (Pulido, 2016, 2017). Discourses of racial capitalism frame problems as racially derived (for instance, resulting from a supposed culture of dysfunctional families in Black communities), rather than systemic (for instance, resulting from the grievous impacts of poverty, segregation and school-to-prison pipelines that are frequently the lived realities of Black communities). These are discursive formations that often employ territorial stigmatization to spatialize differences in the urban experience. As Loyd and

Bonds (2018) explain, rather than appreciating the ways that these issues are interconnected with racialized wealth and privilege, stigmatized communities are often positioned as "lost causes," subjected to exploitation, disinvestment and abandonment. Racial injustices produce uneven environmental conditions across cities, and these in turn track to deepened marginalities, for instance, through troublesome patterns of elevated asthma caused by the poorer air quality in communities of colour. This urge for "mapping" racialized people in cities, which is prominent across academic disciplines, can be deeply harmful, even when purportedly serving to advance equity and justice since it often reinforces territorial stigmatization and biased assumptions about residents. Katherine McKittrick (2021) emphasizes that such conceptualization "reifies the absoluteness of space and casts it as an empty container, thus naturalizing uneven geographies and their attendant social inequities" (10).

Resistance to the structures upholding racial capitalism is largely rooted in an ethic of care, healing and reparation, offering a foundation for more just and sustainable futures. Encouraging attentiveness to the everyday and mundane, Walter Hood (2020) advocates for the commemoration of the "vernacular past" as a means of validating Black landscapes and Black lifeways. Hood's approach to care is cast through historic correction as an investment in the future:

> Black landscapes matter because they are renewable. We can uncover, exhume, validate, and celebrate these landscapes through new narratives and stories that choose to return us to origins. The contested and the forgotten landscapes, renewed through myriad of expressions, can give us incentives to obligations for years to come.
>
> *(4)*

Rinaldo Walcott's (2021) *On Property* describes the necessary transformation as abolition, exposing the violence of capital as Black degradation, disposability and death. He focuses on wellbeing and couples ethical and political commitments through the construction of property, especially in terms of the evolving and lasting impacts of the property regimes of slavery on Black people through "bodily theft, land theft, genocide and near genocide, primitive accumulation, capitalism, and so on" (104). Walcott urges a shift from private property (and the police and carceral systems formed to protect it) to a shared commons:

> Since what historians have called the enclosure of the commons, where monarchies in Europe appropriate specific lands for their use and benefit, the commons as both an idea and a practical means of organizing life has consistently been reduced to private property. A renewed idea of the commons for our times brings along with it a different idea of care, too, including for the earth itself. Stewardship is an essential aspect of abolition, and in this instance would include collective responsibility for our shared resources as a basis for how we care for each other. Those resources are not only the earth; they also include the world's technological and accumulated wealth, accrued through more than five hundred years of exploitation of many of us. The realization

of this vision of the commons necessitates a profound shift in how we understand life, and abolition is the name we give this wish for transformation.

(95)

Axel González's (2019) examination of key strains of racial capitalism illuminates the union of deindustrialization, unemployment, colonialism, health crises, prison toxicity and extractive imperialism, and how these merge into the production of nature. He explains that

> racial capitalism can be understood as a way to organize nature in which, for example, oil that travels in pipelines through Indigenous nations and sacred sites is later processed in refineries located disproportionately in poor communities of color, lighting the fumes of capital accumulation amid ecological and social destruction.
>
> *(1157)*

Similarly, work on abolitionist climate justice [for instance, Ranganathan and Bratman (2021) and McGee and Greiner (2020)] locates the fossil fuel industry as a nexus of capitalist oppression arising from slavery and colonialism. The devaluing of bodies that are not white is deeply ingrained in socio-economic and legal legacies that produce structural advantages and entitlements for white people, and infusion of these legacies into contemporary urban environmental experiences is unmistakable. Malini Ranganathan (2016) explains how white supremacy is naturalized racial capitalism through, noting that

> White supremacy is not simply the material privileges (e.g. clean drinking water, no living near a highway, green spaces, etc.) that subtly accrue on the basis of a system that invariably favors white skin. As a concept, white supremacy also embeds a historiography of how racial hierarchy came to be – how it was instated as an organizing, taken-for-granted logic.
>
> *(21)*

This taken-for-granted logic that inequitably apportions value and entitlement is further enacted through multi-faceted oppressions that permeate urban ecological systems.

The research and thought of queer ecologies also offer fertile analytical insight of direct relevance to urban political ecology. Queer ecologies' critiques of Western cultural dichotomization of nature and culture and heteronormative projections of ecology are particularly enriching avenues of inquiry into the ecological expression of urban politics. As Schnabel (2014) summarizes, queer ecologies reveal

> the ways we read normalized Western heteronormative subjectivities into nature, treating it as an object over which we have alleged god-given domination, misunderstanding its queerness and the ways in which nature potentiates, and even constitutes, both human and animal subjects.
>
> *(12)*

Dispelling ecological orthodoxies of heterosexuality (for instance, that mating is uniquely in service of procreation or that queer behaviour in nonhumans is unnatural) allows for more ambiguity, complexity and indeterminacy in our interpretations of nature, which effectually render our interpretations more accurate. Alex Johnson (2011) characterizes queer ecology as liberatory ecology, "the study of dynamics across all phenomena, all behavior, all possibilities" and "acknowledgement of the numberless relations between all things alive, once alive, and alive once again." Foundational works include Mortimer-Sandilands and Erikson's (2010) edited collection on heteronormative ecological agendas and Patrick's (2014) ecological queering of New York City's waterfront and High Line. Gandy's (2012b) heterotopic analysis of urban nature through technical surveillance, natural surveillance, queer cruising, death, nocturnal public culture and unruly spaces advances Lefebvre's right to the city, affirming "how different kinds of cultural or political alliances might emerge in relation to the protection of specific sites" (740). Reflecting on queerness of the natural world, Lupino-Smith (2018) recounts

> I have come to realize that some of the places where urban coyotes can thrive without detection and queer folks can hook up are the same. We share these spaces because they both need the wild within the city. It's a wild that exists in the places and spaces that are liminal, nestled in-between the order of the developed urban landscape.

Anti-colonial and decolonial ecological perspectives on cities may further enlighten urban political ecology, not only in terms of critiquing how cities and nature are structured by coloniality but also as an overdue interruption of Western research practices and paradigms. Studies exploring Indigenous struggles for sovereignty [for instance, Tomiak (2017), McGregor et al. (2020) and McMillen et al. (2020)] amid settler-colonialism illustrate vital socio-ecological interventions in urban settings, particularly in terms of approaching equity and justice in ways that meaningfully challenge the momentum of urbanized capitalism. Laying out the taken-for-granted logic of racial capitalism and heteronormativity, Glen Coulthard (2014), a member of the Yellowknives Dene First Nation, characterizes settler-colonialism as "territorially acquisitive in perpetuity" and reasons that it "should not be seen as deriving its reproductive force solely from its strictly repressive or violent features, but rather from its ability to produce *forms of* life that make settler-colonialism's constitutive hierarchies seem natural" (152, emphasis in original). These concerns also resonate in reflections on the analytical inadequacy of conceptual approaches rooted in the Global North for understanding realities in the rest of the world [for instance, Noxolo (2017)]. Red River Métis-Michif scholar Max Liboiron's (2021) *Pollution is Colonialism*, for example, argues that a proper understanding of pollution does not conceptualize it as environmental damage, but rather as symptoms of the violence of colonial relations. Highlighting the analytical approach of the Civic Laboratory for Environmental Action Research (a marine science lab that focuses on anti-colonial land relations), Liboiron explains how "bad relations" of colonialism allow pollution to occur through territorial entitlements that assimilate pollution into land itself. This mode of thinking, where land serves as a sink for unwanted matter, is replete in the formation of cities across North America and the diverse forms of colonialism, particularly in terms of industrial production as a primary form of capital accumulation. Scholars such as Coulthard (2014) argue strongly in favour of the strategies for place-based practices that are rooted in specific Indigenous values that are self-affirming and challenge the colonial subjectivities produced through the liberal politics of recognition and the structures of settler-colonial power.

An anti-colonial political ecology seeks to dismantle colonial norms around life and liberate Indigenous space for Indigenous determination. For non-Indigenous people, Leanne Betasamosake Simpson (2017), a member of the Alderville First Nation, explains that this means getting out of the way so Indigenous knowledge, theory, resistance, resurgence and sustenance can thrive on Indigenous nations' own terms. Simpson elucidates,

> Indigenous peoples with radical imaginations and desires for freedom must create collective, private physical spaces where we come together and think very long and hard about how to organize and build resurgent movements, about how we move beyond everyday acts of resurgence to collective actions in the short and long term, and about how to create community that embodies and practices our nation-based processes in the present.
>
> *(234)*

Liboiron's (2021) elaboration of anti-colonial methods for science pertains directly to urban political ecology. Examples include prioritizing nuanced connections with specific places, rejecting universalism and not reproducing settler-colonial entitlements to Indigenous land, cultures, concepts and lifeworlds. As broadly defined "decolonial" approaches to knowledge, thinking and political structures are increasingly absorbed into mainstream rhetoric; Tuck and Yang (2012) hold that the goals and practices of decolonization must be recognized distinctly, not melded into broader anti-oppression approaches. Arguing that simply decentring whiteness is incommensurate with decolonization, they explain that

> Decolonization, which we assert is a distinct project from other civil and human rights-based social justice projects, is far too often subsumed into the directives of these projects, with no regard for how decolonization wants something different than those forms of justice.
>
> *(2)*

A dearth of anti-colonial and decolonial foci in urban political ecology has led to blind spots concerning settler-colonial processes as historical and ongoing dispossession and erasure, including through the formation and management of greenspaces. As Simpson and Bagelman (2018) point out, this omission risks reproducing uncritical colonial discourses within the field of urban political ecology itself. They draw attention to ways that racial capitalism fortifies settler-colonialism and emphasize the everyday acts of urban Indigenous people connected to ancestral lands and management practices. Simpson (2017) identifies queer indigeneity as a crucial expression of Indigenous brilliance that generates land-based resurgence and alternatives to dispossession, the forces of capitalism, white supremacy and heteropatriarchy. This is a critical part of the "embedded processes as freedom" (17) that Simpson advocates as strategic departures from the structures of settler-colonialism.

Re-Sistering is an edifying project that brings these themes together through re-Indigenizing and placekeeping work in Toronto while creating a welcoming environment for two-spirit people.[1] It includes a garden and medicine earthworks on ancestral sites along Niwa'ah Onega'gaih'ih – Kobechenonk (the Humber River). Garden Coordinator Joce Two Crows Tremblay, who is a member of the Indigenous Land Stewardship Circle and founder of the Sweet Grass Collective, describes the careful preliminary work of convening monthly with elders to realize the vision for returning the lands and traditions as part of a two-spirit mission (Finding Flowers, 2021). From the onset, the Re-Sistering project focused on re-storying the area through an approach that Two Crows calls spirit work, as deep de-colonial work to revive spirits in a safe way based on long-term relationships with ancestors. In 2017, for instance, a group of over 60 two-spirit people gathered in canoes to experience a shadow puppet show animating the river's history by the artist collective Drawing With Knives, followed by a feast. The project endured a major setback in June 2019 when, only days after the release of the *Final Report of the National Inquiry Into Missing and Murdered Indigenous Women and Girls* (NIM-MIWG, 2019), City of Toronto employees destroyed ceremonial items and the Three Sisters garden that was planted by Indigenous community members working with the Ojibiikaan's Two-Spirit Families Circle (Muskrat Magazine, 2019). The community was horrified. They gathered to light a sacred fire to grieve the garden's destruction, received donations of Hopi tobacco from members of the Toronto Black Farmers Collective and set up camp on site for 21 days (Finding Flowers, 2021). Then they replanted the garden. Projects like Re-Sistering offer responses to the genocide and displacement of Indigenous people that are based on deepened relationships with histories, identities and living systems, emphasizing ancestral teachings and shared relationships with the land and water. These decolonial perspectives encompass multi-generations timelines based on reciprocity and care, producing socio-ecological interventions in urban settings that confound the violence of colonial relations through place-based practices prioritizing nuanced connections and Indigenous resurgence.

Urban ecosystems as novel ecosystems

Diverse readings of the urban notwithstanding, whether they are decried as indications of degradation or celebrated as living systems, there is little debate about the persistence of ecological processes in urban settings. Yet, interpretations with credibility in the natural and physical sciences tend to insufficiently address the socio-political dimensions of urbanization. Sharpening awareness of the biophysical dimensions of urban ecology is also overdue in the social sciences. Arguing that social sciences can help resolve the overwhelming struggle of the natural and physical sciences to interpret what constitutes urban space, McIntyre et al. (2000) detail how "demographic, economic, political, perceptive, and cultural criteria, when used in conjunction with geophysical and biological criteria, provide a more complete and useful definition" than permitted within the confines of physical and natural sciences. The shortcomings of any singular approach can only be addressed through awareness of what is going on in other fields, and any meaningful interpretation of urban ecology demands a high level of interdisciplinarity.

A number of ecological principles stand out as particularly pertinent to understanding post-industrial urban greenspace. Landscape ecologist Richard Forman (2016) presents a synthesis of ninety succinct principles, none of which "would have emerged from research on natural areas, and all are readily usable for improving urban and urbanizing areas" (1653). Qualitatively dissimilar to the principles applied in non-urban areas, these principles shed light on the distinct ecological processes that characterize the spaces within which the majority of humans live worldwide. They affirm that cities have elevated levels of biodiversity, with high habitat diversity created by the very buildings and tall structures that distinguish urban from peri-urban, rural and "semi-natural" settings. These claims are substantiated through research demonstrating that environmental generalists tend to predominate urban ecosystems, and species populations exhibit high mortality and depend on replenishment from the surrounding semi-natural areas. Cities are distinctly warmer than surrounding regions and are primary CO_2 emitters. They have longer growing and flowering periods, and seed dispersal is assisted by human mobility, stormwater runoff and the accelerated airflow incited by built structures. Pulses of new species prompt rapid changes to overall species composition and abundance. Urban wildlife tends to tolerate and communicate incessant noise, and many species avoid people and traffic with nocturnal cycles of activity and rest. Streets and roadways function as both conduits and barriers to movement. Soils are highly variable in width and depth, with high concentrations of heavy metals, pesticides and other organic compounds.

In relation to chemicals and organisms, Forman notes that "Cities are cauldrons of countless human-created chemicals, overwhelmingly with unknown effects on species and their biology" (1658). Water tables tend to be lower than surrounding areas, wetlands are scarce and stormwater runoff dominates water flows, causing fluctuations in water levels and pollutant concentrations. Streams are often truncated, channelized with hard banks or buried. Species movement along green corridors tends to be limited, and wildlife travels along "stepping stone" routes composed of smaller greenspaces in proximity. Interestingly, informal human settlements are likely to produce higher biodiversity than more intensively maintained sites, and all major transportation modes (ships, trains, airplanes and road vehicles) continually convey non-native species into cities, which then disperse.

These constitute a mere sample of the principles that specifically correspond with post-industrial spaces, and they must always be considered within a broad range of urban variables and regional socio-political dynamics.

Pickett and Cadenasso (2017) offer a different, yet complementary, set of principles that are deductively oriented. In contrast to Forman's comprehensive list of 90 principles drawn from empirical induction, Pickett and Cadenasso suggest five "metaprinciples," broken down into a subset of thirteen generalized principles that are more useful for urban designers and landscape architects. They point out that Forman's inductive findings are biased towards the Global North, specifically in terms of baseline conditions that are less relevant in the Global South, such as the industrial revolution and urban planning models that idealize hygiene and sanitation. Key differences notwithstanding, the two approaches are highly compatible, enriching knowledge of urban ecology as distinct from other ecologies in less densely inhabited settings.

TABLE 2.1 Pickett and Cadenasso's (2017) 13 principles of urban ecology

1	Cities and urban areas are human ecosystems in which social-economic and ecological processes feed back to one another
2	Urban areas contain remnant or newly emerging vegetated and stream patches that exhibit ecological functions
3	Urban flora and fauna are diverse, and this diversity has multiple dimensions (e.g. taxonomy, phylogenetics, function and geographic origin)
4	Human values and perceptions are a key link mediating the feedback between social and ecological components of human ecosystems
5	Ecological processes are differentially distributed across the metropolis, and the limitation of services and excess of hazards is often associated with the location of human communities that are poor, discriminated against or otherwise disempowered
6	Urban form is heterogeneous on many scales, and fine-scale heterogeneity is especially notable in cities and older suburbs
7	Urban form reflects planning, incidental and indirect effects of social and environmental decisions
8	Urban form is a dynamic phenomenon and exhibits contrasts through time and across regions that express different cultural and economic contexts of urbanization
9	Urban designs and development projects at various scales can be treated as experiments and used to expose the ecological effects of different design and management strategies
10	Definition of the boundaries and content of an urban system model is set by the researchers based on their research questions or the spatial scope of its intended application
11	Urban comparisons can be framed as linear transects or as abstract gradients, and the abstract comparisons acknowledge the spatial complexity of urban heterogeneity
12	Urban land covers and land uses extend into and interdigitate with rural or wild land covers and uses
13	The flux of water, including both clean water supply, waste, and stormwater management, is of concern to urban and urbanizing areas worldwide and connects them explicitly to larger regions

By investing in a deeper understanding of how organisms (including humans) interact in their environments, we are also investing in our own ability to make informed decisions about which natural features, which types of relationships and which ecological processes we will nurture. Clearly, urban ecosystems are worthy of serious consideration in their own right, not just as tarnished versions of the time-honoured "proper" ecosystems that remain the primary preoccupation of scientists and naturalists. Since the patterns and processes of urban ecosystems are distinct from unsettled, rural or less cultivated landscapes, we cannot simply transpose the principles from other ecological fields directly onto urban systems. Commitment to life forms in cities requires moving beyond simplistic notions of nature and the limitations of singular disciplinary perspectives, since the physical attributes of urban spaces – for instance, compacted soils, dense particulate, relentless noise, dumpsters full of food waste, asphalt, skyscrapers and culverted water systems – create particular ecological conditions that are socio-ecological and demand far more than generalized or vague conceptions of nature as a category that stands for everything non-human. Understanding, for example, how seeds disperse through urban rail lines, how wastewater sites and dumps become wildlife refuges or how soil quality is affected by historic land uses allows us to think more clearly about the equitable distribution of ecological assets and deficits. It is a commitment to understanding how humans are always participating in the formation of ecological habitat even when we are not paying attention.

Being attentive to the specifics of urban ecology also disabuses us of the custodial and managerial roles that many assume humans occupy in relation to natural environments, where we have ultimate responsibility for ecological wellbeing, since it quickly becomes apparent that we are immersed in mutually dependent relationships and do not have authority over nature, including in heavily settled environments. And it also becomes clear that we must set aside generic conceptions of nature because they blind us to the reality that cities are almost entirely composed of novel ecosystems that do not correspond with the prototypes typifying conventional ecological classifications. This is to say that as we adopt more ecologically sophisticated interpretations of nature in cities, we commit more and more to the possibilities of self-sustaining ecological assemblages that do not observe historical precedents. As Alexis Shotwell (2016) points out in *Against Purity*, "living in a disturbance regime means that we are all living after events that have changed, and frequently harmed, ecosystems and biospheres. Change is not the same thing as harm, and harm is unevenly distributed" (9).

Although not unique to urban environments, novel ecosystems dominate cities. They are the product of colonization and resilience, both symptoms of degradation and material evidence of recovery. These ecological expressions are, as Eric Higgs (2017) notes, "rooted in the processes of human transformation" (12). They are the results of inadvertent human activities, nature reconstituting itself amid the vestiges of human-induced ecological alterations that either directly or indirectly transform the relationships between biotic and abiotic elements. As new combinations of species form relationships without historic precedents, the novel ecosystems that emerge are unfamiliar within classical conceptions of ecology. Perhaps most notably, there are no climax communities, and notions of native, exotic and invasive species become irrelevant to assessments of environmental quality.

The concept of novel ecosystems is new in itself. Although the idea of species evolving into relationships devoid of reference systems has probably been understood since the nascence of ecology as a field of study, the term novel ecosystems was coined by Chapin and Starfield (1997) to articulate the shifting arctic treeline in the Alaskan tundra. A decade later, Hobbs et al. (2006) challenged conventional ecological discourse with the proposition of "emerging ecosystems" that "can be thought of as occupying a zone somewhere in the middle of the gradient between 'natural' or 'wild' ecosystems, on the one hand, and intensively managed systems on the other hand" (2). This was disturbing to many. Fred Pearce (2015) remarks that novel ecosystems do not comply with most conservationists' "paradigm of how nature is organized" and "complicate their wish to protect and revive nature by excluding a wide range of options for reviving the wild" (156). He describes how this is a profoundly difficult worldview for some, explaining that "The recognition that novel ecosystems are the future – the new wild – is often painful for conservationists" (161). But for post-industrial urban greenspace, where historical references are often buried and are always deeply altered, where environmental conditions bear no similarity to those that preceded industrialization, novel ecosystems are the norm. In fact, they present vital life options that are anything but degraded, working against the legacy of industrial harm to renew life.

Novel ecosystems are self-sustaining and indeterminate, not the product of design. As Miller and Bestelmeyer (2016) eloquently argue, "a novel ecosystem is not an alternate state of the system, but a decision" (578). By this, they mean that novel ecosystems correspond with choices not to actively engineer the pattern and processes of a space. These ecosystems are notable in that they do not overtly serve human interests. Nor do they respond to human goals, and they do not actuate direct benefits for humans. They are the product of disregard, either intentional or unintentional. They are sparingly managed, if at all. Designed ecosystems may eventually become novel ecosystems, for instance, where a park becomes overgrown and inaccessible to humans or the perennial garden in a vacant urban lot succeeds into woody shrubland. However, designed systems are organized to primarily serve humans. Hybrid ecosystems are distinct from novel ones in that they have been extensively altered but bear continuity with historic biotic and abiotic features (Hobbs et al., 2014). Higgs (2017) provides a useful profile of novel ecosystems in relation to the practice of restoration ecology as habitat creation and offers a template for conceptualizing ecosystem as either self-assembled or designed. He is careful to note that the distinctions are imperfect, commenting that

> In each case, the characterization is open to debate and counterexamples can be easily presented. For example, restored ecosystems are usually managed for ecological integrity but there are also many examples where sustained cultural practices (harvesting, burning) are prominent or manifest distinctly cultural values (e.g. aesthetic features in the case of many urban restoration projects).

(11)

TABLE 2.2 Self-assembling and designed ecosystems, adapted from Higgs (2017)

Type of Ecosystem		Degree of Intervention	Ongoing Management	Historicity	Management Intervention
Self-assembling	Historical	None – negligible	None–low	Strong	Ecosystem-centred
	Restored	Low	Low	Strong	Ecosystem-centred
	Hybrid	Low–moderate	Low–moderate	Moderate-strong	Ecosystem-centred
	Novel	Low	Low	Low–moderate	Ecosystem-centred
Designed	Reclaimed	Moderate-heavy	Variable–low	Low	Human-centred
	Green infrastructure	Heavy	Variable–heavy	Low	Human-centred
	Agroecology	Variable, intensive	Variable, moderate	Variable, low	Human-centred

Some researchers and practitioners are unenthusiastic about novel ecosystems, since the concept is theoretical rather than evidentiary. For instance, Kattan et al. (2016) argue that the term's imprecision renders it "fuzzy" and universal, and thus of little pragmatic value. They explain that "it serves no classifying purpose," "presents no specific set of principles from which testable predications can be derived" and does not "inform a practical framework because it offers nothing concrete for decision-making or management" (716). However, others such as Kowarik and von der Lippe (2018) point out that as they mature, novel ecosystems provide habitat for native and endangered plant species, and that understanding the habitat functions of natural remnant, hybrid and novel ecosystems helps identify opportunities and set priorities for biodiversity conservation across all urban ecosystems. Emma Marris (2010), likewise, emphasizes the scientific merit of research on novel ecosystems as highly dynamic environments that demonstrate the forces of succession and change, pointing out

> Novel ecosystems are often ideal natural experiments for studying things such as community assembly – how species find their way to a place and which species become permanent residents – and evolution of species in response to one another. In essence, it takes a dynamic ecosystem to study ecosystem dynamics, and these novel ecosystems are the planet's fastest movers.

One point upon which both sides agree is the need for a case-by-case approach to understanding how novel ecosystems operate and who inhabits them, since typologies are irrelevant (Murcia et al., 2014; Miller & Bestelmeyer, 2016). And perhaps most poignantly in terms of resisting the precepts of orthodox ecological wisdom that plague urban ecosystems, there is also general agreement that the term has a high value in shedding the heavy baggage of the term "degraded" and facilitating recognition of the ecological vibrancy of urban settings. This in turn elevates appreciation of post-industrial urban spaces, particularly spaces that have been disregarded and have gone wild in their own unique ways, including ways that might not correspond with conventional aesthetic ideals of what greenspaces should resemble, who should inhabit them and what constitutes urban sustainability. Refuting the classification of these spaces as degraded and appreciating them as novel welcomes new suites of possible futures, based on decision-making criteria that do not idealize the pristine, unsullied and preserved, but instead value investment in the nature that permeates cities.

Environmental justice

Environmental justice is at the core of any meaningful interpretation of urban sustainability. By centring equity through considerations such as differential exposure to toxins, the distribution of environmental stressors, uneven participation in civic processes and the expression of systemic racism across urban landscapes, environmental justice provides a lens through which the social mediation of ecological systems must be understood and acted upon. Yet, most urban ecological research fails to foreground these concerns, and there is a fissure between studies that are biophysically focused (for instance, on air quality issues like particulate measures) and those that emphasize urban social justice concerns (for instance, the cultural politics of representation). Environmental justice research, thought and action connect biophysical realities of urban matters with lived experiences to understand and address uneven access to the environmental quality of life. Teelucksingh et al. (2016) identify the field's strength in the provision of a "structural framework to analyse the power relations between different environmental and social stakeholders, as well as to make connections between broader macro-level processes and the needs of marginalized communities" (383). The research and practice of environmental justice are dynamic, holding the most promise among the many approaches to urban sustainability for challenging the destructive and harmful momentum of capitalism on human lives and ecosystems.

The field of environmental justice is well established and growing. Agyeman et al. (2003) describe the field's inception as concern about the interwoven challenges of lack of access for minority groups to decision- and policy-making processes and the disproportionate share of environmental detriments to which these same communities are exposed. Effects may include problems such as imperilled health, insufficient infrastructure, inferior access to and less enjoyment of common and open spaces, substandard housing and climate-related issues like flooding and exposure to extreme temperatures. Experiencing these effects can heighten the barriers to participation in decision-making processes, compounding marginalization. Environmental injustices span the range of landscape types and settlement patterns, and cycles of environmental injustice travel across political and geographic boundaries. Environmental justice considerations are relevant in any environmental phenomenon and can be identified in all areas of environmental engagement.

An effective illustration of the saturation of environmental justice concerns is scholarship in the "geographies of waste" (Gregson & Crang, 2010; Millington & Lawhon, 2019), a field examining multi-scalar processes and material imprints enacted through global flows of industrial by-products. Moore (2012) summarizes some of the interlacing dynamics as

> a billion dollar industry in hazardous waste trade; expanding interests in and uses of alternative practices of waste management; large-scale development institutions' investment in waste-related infrastructure in the developing world; increasing subnational transfers of municipal solid waste; and growing piles of e-waste overwhelming local dumpsites, to name a few.
>
> *(780)*

By focusing on the concept of "waste formations" as the fusion of the processes of waste, space and race, Lindsey Dillon (2014) reveals how waste participates in racial formations to channel the experience of twentieth-century American cities, and how race signifies the "waste-ability of urban space" and the wasting of human lives through proximity between environmental hazards and racialized bodies. Within this context, work that focuses on matters such as e-waste in places like Accra (Akese & Little, 2018; Amuzu, 2018) helps shed light on the pluralities of environmental injustices that are activated, demonstrating how justice can mean very different things in different circumstances and from different perspectives.

In post-industrial urban greenspace, the production of environmental injustices is always operative. As sites become disused, their legacies of contamination, hazard and disinvestment are amplified, and this is experienced primarily by those living in proximity. In most instances in the Global North, proximity to industrial operations coincides with patterns of settlement by people who are working-class or economically disadvantaged, people of colour, newcomers leaving unsafe or impoverished homelands and people who have experienced intergenerational marginalization. When the factories, dumps, rail lines or infrastructural utilities close down, the cumulative environmental deficits remain. These spaces often become categorized (both by custom or in official records) as urban vacancies that are unmanaged. They typically develop the outward appearance of dilapidation and neglect, commonly interpreted as clear signals of neighbourhood blight that reinforce the dangerous and unpleasant quality of the community at large. Living in proximity to such space can mean living with daily reminders that one's community is unworthy of care and protection from toxins, that contaminated soil, water and air are acceptable for certain residents to experience and that urban investments are destined for more desirable neighbourhoods.

Environmental justice is best understood through the experiences, actions and strategies of those seeking to improve their communities, and responding to damage is never solely about the biophysical environment. Especially in urban settings, these struggles are not just focused on decontaminating soil and cleaning air. They involve strategic coalitions among varied interests to simultaneously address interconnected challenges like low-quality and unaffordable housing, food scarcity, unemployment and poverty alongside the quest for improved health outcomes, a clean environment and accessible open space. As Isabelle Anguelovski (2014) remarks, "socioenvironmental endeavours and the narratives that activists built around their projects heal grief, decrease loss and violence, create safe havens and refuges, celebrate the neighbourhood, and ultimately remake a place and home for residents" (25). She describes how the larger political vision of historically excluded groups is often about remaking local places through both anguish and hope, based on attachments to these places. Pushing against generalized urban political ecology interpretations, Anguelovski points out that "Beyond claiming a right to the city, they claim a right to their neighbourhood" (27). While some urban political ecology research underestimates local actors' appreciation of the complexity of socio-ecological interactions, and environmental justice literature has a tendency to focus on severe and high-impact sources of harm and inequity, emerging work illuminates the commonplace sources and continuing conditions that enable injustice in people's everyday lives (Hornik et al., 2016).

Some of the earliest renowned cases of environmental injustice in urban settings involved severe and unmistakable health crises for people living and working near toxic waste. One of the first to attract widespread attention was in the Love Canal neighbourhood of Niagara Falls, New York, where the burial of over 22,000 tons of 80 toxic chemicals, including known carcinogens such as benzene, caused severe physical harm and cognitive impairment for residents. This was a working-class and low-income community of approximately 1,000 homes, a mix of single-family and apartment residences. After decades of living, working, learning and recreating amid chemicals buried in the local canal, in the late 1970s, residents began organizing to draw attention to inflated rates of congenital disabilities and anomalies, seizures, intellectual and learning disabilities, miscarriages and crib deaths, stunted growth among children, urinary tract disorders and mental illness, among other concerning health conditions (CHEJ, 2015); 30% of residents had experienced chromosomal damage (Babcock, 1980), and 56% of children born between 1974 and 1978 had anomalies such as three ears or double rows of teeth (CHEJ, 2015). In terms of public discourse and knowledge production, the protest leaders who attracted widespread publicity were depicted as newly politicized white working-class homemakers. But these women were actually part of a broader coalition that was less apparent in news cycles. The coalition included Christian groups, Black women and the NAACP (National Association for the Advancement of Colored People) civil rights organization fighting to ensure that the Black residents were not left behind when white residents were relocated out of Love Canal (Blum, 2008; Hay, 2009). The contamination of the Love Canal community is a despicable instance of environmental injustice, but the additional marginalization of the health and safety of Black residents attests to the particular ways that race combines with poverty to magnify harm, as well as the ease with which the leadership of communities of colour could be obscured. Before long, in the early-1980s, national attention turned to a poor Black community in Warren County, North Carolina, that was resisting a toxic waste disposal facility proposed for siting in their vicinity. In this case, the racially disproportionate impact of environmental toxicity was unmistakable, as was the institutionalized racial discrimination in land usage policy (Bullard, 2000; McGurty, 2007). Although the waste disposal facility was eventually erected in Warren County, this was the case that helped crystalize environmental justice as the melding of distributive and procedural equity through the environmental concerns that have real and lasting impacts on people's lives, particularly the lives of people of colour.

The social determinants of health are at the root of the contemporary environmental justice movement, especially in terms of the ways that urban spaces are racially structured and how this intersects with class, gender, ablism, sexuality and other mechanisms of hierarchical division. When serious health issues such as asthma, hypertension and diabetes become common in low-income communities of colour, they usually can be linked to urban planning decisions about siting toxic land uses like factories and dumps, as well as perilous infrastructure like highways that both constrain communities and expose them to elevated levels of pollution. Dillon and Sze (2016) trace how these problems are amplified by state security practices of surveillance, particularly in terms of breath, policing and air quality. They build off McKittrick's (2006) analysis of Black geographies as geographic patterns characterized by displacement, marginalization and eradication of Black lives, the inscription of Black bodies in and out of spaces and the erasure of Black knowledge and expertise. Dillon and Sze interpret the emergence of the phrase "I can't breathe" as constitutive of state-sanctioned violence, racial health disparities and the environmental justice movement, explaining that "the inability to breathe can be understood as both a metaphor and material reality of racism, which constrains not just life choices and opportunities, but the environmental conditions of life itself" (19).

In terms of industrial activities, the community of Hunts Point in South Bronx, New York City, provides a poignant illustration of the ways that specific low-income communities of colour are negatively impacted while these same communities must struggle to participate in the decision-making processes affecting their neighbourhoods. In *Noxious New York*, Julie Sze (2006) provides a profile of environmental health activism in response to the health harms of intense industrial activity. In 2000, 75.8% of residents in Hunt's Point identified as Latino and 21.4% identified as Black (or African-American Nonhispanic, in the codification of the US Census Bureau), 42.7% were supported by social assistance and 90.1% lived in rental units. This has long been the poorest congressional district in the United States, which for decades endured high crime rates and housing decline due to abandonment or arson, often ignited by landlords anticipating insurance claims (Meyerson, 2015). In the 1990s, after a medical waste incinerator was constructed right in the neighbourhood, a coalition of community groups successfully organized to shut it down and destroy the smokestack that had released fumes into the neighbourhood. In eight years of operation, the incinerator had garnered over 500 violations for toxic releases. Community groups such as the South Bronx Clean Air Coalition and the POINT Community Development Corporation continued to organize and resist the addition of toxic facilities in their neighbourhood, such as a paper recycling plant and a marine-to-rail waste transfer facility, by mobilizing residents, participating in hearings and suing administrative bodies (Sze, 2006). But in Hunts Point heavy trucks ceaselessly travel along a latticework of transportation infrastructure servicing the largest food distribution hub in the world and over 15 waste transfer stations, in addition to a disproportionate share of regional heavy industry. These conditions have caused public health epidemics in the community, for instance, around asthma, diabetes and obesity. Residents continued to fight for environmental justice. Groups like Sustainable South Bronx and Youth Ministries for Peace and Justice lobbied and fundraised through the early 2000s to clean up the Bronx River and address the dearth of neighbourhood green spaces (Brotchner, 2014). Eventually, they succeeded in converting old industrial sites into community assets like Hunts Point Riverside Park, Barretto Point Park and Concrete Plant Park. Residents participated in designing these public parks to reflect the history of the neighbourhood and provide space for community gathering, recreation and river access. Notably, these successes in Hunts Point were guided not just by the desire to redress environmental damage. These are visions of environmental justice that are just as much about creating jobs, improving people's living conditions, advancing academic and political education, advocating for holistic approaches to health and wellness and creating opportunities for the local community to shape its own aesthetic environment through arts and public engagement in community design. They are part of a broad overall urban sustainability strategy by residents to claim their community and demand that it reflects their own self-defined goals and desires. This animation of Lefebvre's right to the city – which is defined through citizenship (as inhabitation, not formal status or documentation), participation (making decisions about space) and appropriation (occupying and creating space) – through socio-environmental production in South Bronx asserted the residents' ascendency in helping recompose the urban metabolism of their own community. Residents were not interested in leaving their perilous, aesthetically unsavoury community. They were interested in cleaning it up and shaping it according to their own ideals and aesthetic preferences while reversing the momentum of urban inequity.

Environmental aesthetics

Environmental aesthetics are about far more than the experience of nature arranged into beautiful compositions. They are about the quality of life. Yuriko Saito (2008) concisely defines aesthetics as "any reactions we form toward the sensuous and/ or design qualities of any object, phenomenon or activity" (9). She insists on the primacy of "everyday aesthetics" as the experiential interface most deeply affecting people's relationships with their surroundings. Rejecting art-centred conceptions of aesthetics that focus on composition and authorial intent as well as standards for evaluation, she argues that these lead to the "special experiences" approach that obfuscates the subtleties and ecological qualities of commonplace surroundings. Moreover, the "special experiences" approach does not stimulate actions that support long-term environmental sustainability. Similarly, Saito refutes Western hierarchical aesthetic interpretations in favour of openness to diverse ways of engaging with diverse phenomenon. By prioritizing appreciation of and investment in the everyday aesthetics that shape unremarkable human experiences in home environments and ordinary settings, she argues, aesthetic preferences can be infused with ecological literacy and imaginative capacities to form meaningful land-based relationships, and these attachments and affections can be environmentally enriching. This is an approach that centres quotidian surroundings as the locus for creating a sense of place, shaped not by experts or taste-makers but by and for those who experience them most directly. Saito explains:

> There is a pressing need to cultivate aesthetic literacy, so to speak, with respect to everyday objects and environment. By doing so, we can become more aware of how the power of everyday aesthetic is instrumental in steering our actions and societies' policies in a certain direction, sometimes toward problematic ends such as environmental irresponsibility or dubious political agenda while other times toward positive goals such as creation of a humane and environmentally sound world for everyone. Everyday aesthetic, I firmly believe, has to be a part of the strategies for the project of world-making, to which all of us in some way participate, both personally and professionally, sometimes quite consciously and some other times unwittingly.
>
> *(243)*

An affective interpretation of aesthetics appreciates the multi-sensory experience that engages whole bodies, not just the visual senses that tend to be privileged in Western aesthetic traditions. This means that aesthetics, like ecologies, are immersive and inescapable, always activated. The range of responses is infinite, not merely positive or negative, and can include powerful sentiments such as fear, wonder or curiosity. Responses can also be banal or uninspiring. These are emotional responses, and aesthetics can call upon the entire repertoire of a person's past experiences, some of which may be singular and subjectively interpreted. As immersive experiences of one's surroundings, environmental aesthetics are also bodily encounters that are deeply personal. For instance, the emotional impact of spending a day hearing, smelling and feeling a dark, damp forest without clear sight lines has a profoundly individual and different neurological effect and lasting imprint than the experiences of swimming along a warm tropical shoreline, playing volleyball indoors, tracking a meadow landscape from a train window, watching a nature program while folding laundry or meditating on a starry panoramic skyline. And the neurology, memory and interpretation of each of these experiences will vary dramatically among different people, in spite of the coding of landscape types for safety, cleanliness, beauty and other cultural associations.

There is an immense interplay between what we feel and what we learn. Aesthetic responses are largely cultivated by culturally mediated knowledge, knowledge that accumulates over generations and is emotionally infused. It is thus appropriate to situate aesthetic knowledge within the realm of social practices as something that is shared, performed, trained and shaped collectively. By extension, aesthetic knowledge and the responses we learn produce power dynamics. The emotional animation of this knowledge (which is inescapably incomplete and never impartial) through aesthetic engagement with variegated urban settings produces explanatory stories about the world that shape visions of what is relevant, causal, egregious and proper (Foster, 2009). Environmental experiences, in this sense, are often filtered through social conventions that prescribe what is deemed aesthetically positive, such as the Western landscape typologies of "the sublime" and "the picturesque" (Brady, 2003), which in turn have the power to reproduce through biophysical interventions that ensure they become exemplars of aesthetic propriety. Elevating dominant Western aesthetics as "natural beauty" has the effect of invalidating ecological systems that do not correspond with these landscape prototypes. For instance, favouring the chemically saturated, water-hungry and labour-intensive turf lawn across North America (rooted in aesthetic reproduction of the golf greens of Scotland, England, Ireland and Wales) has displaced rich wetlands, forests, meadows and prairies throughout the world. It also marginalizes alternate conceptions of landscape beauty that correspond with different histories and cultural connections. Moreover, it supplants the Indigenous ecological knowledge and practices that supported these landscapes for millennia prior to settler colonization.

Aesthetic agency, or the political poignancy of aesthetics, is far too often overlooked in urban political ecology. Catherin Dee (2010) insists that "an aesthetic education is inseparable from an ethical and a scientific one" (21) and that design is a collective "act of directed unveiling at the intersection of the material reality of landscaped and all public forms" (24). Natalie Blanc (2012) pairs ethics and aesthetics, describing them as "two sides of the same coin," wherein "the desire for a better life is guided by aesthetic judgement and experience" (151). She locates the ethical dimensions of aesthetics in terms of the ways environmental conditions are shaped to reflect particular ideals, and the emotional qualities that form through experiences in these spaces. Blanc writes,

> Aesthetic discussion opens up a space in which to construct an imaginative framework of reference, a representation of the significant space in which we live and also to which we aspire . . . the local is not simply a question of geography, of a more or less measurable space associated with a given group or society, it is also a question of the multiplicity of emotions and relational networks that the local environment engenders.
>
> *(152)*

The exchange between substantially individual aesthetic responses and culturally accrued knowledge of space is in large part conditioned by emotionally based anticipatory structures that relate to particular histories and socio-political contexts. This is to say that environmental aesthetics congeal the politicization of ecology by fusing the sensory with concepts of social order in ways that are lasting yet difficult to detect. Building off the work of Gadamer (1989), anticipatory structures can simultaneously presuppose particular environmental interpretations as conceptually coherent (as both meaningful and complete) and sensorily substantial (where feelings and instincts are activated). And this is where ecologically precarious and socially unjust environmental decisions can disseminate through aesthetic production and reproduction. Commonly shared expectations concerning normal landscapes, healthy ecosystems, pleasant surroundings and appropriate stylization of spaces are actually expressions of beliefs and claims about reality with profound political implications, particularly when these intersect with notions of who belongs, what constitutes a transgression, where to invest or neglect, what is moral and proper and whose preferences are beautiful. These are the filters that enable environmental aesthetics to function as critical thresholds for urban equity and justice.

Analysis of the mobilization of the concept of landscape continuity on the edges of Toronto illuminates how aesthetics can mediate the socio-political dimensions of ecological decision-making to reinforce cultural and racial inequities by reifying colonial landscape imprints and impeding newcomers from moving in. As a core tenet of landscape ecological theory that has been enshrined in North American and European environmental policy and planning, landscape continuity is key criterion in strategies that determine the disposition of thousands of hectares of land surrounding Toronto, specifically along the Niagara Escarpment to the west and the Oak Ridges Moraine to the north and east. The discourse of self-identified environmentalists who have been instrumental in resisting residential development of these landscapes, however, reveals aesthetic validation of emblems of colonial heritage, which is embedded in a desire to "protect" them from perceived outsiders who do not fit the white settler archetype (Foster, 2009, 2010). Depictions of landscape continuity among this group were remarkably congruent, where biophysical appeals to landscape continuity were transposed into cultural considerations unrelated to ecological principles. While concerns like species migration routes and groundwater reserves might have framed the discourse through institutional processes and proposed scientific rationale for resistance to urban expansion, this discourse also incorporated trepidation around matters such as Punjabi and Mandarin signage, Mediterranean-style architectural features and the purported dexterity of Jewish lawyers representing developers in land-use tribunals. Clearly, ecology was functioning as politics by other means. The rate of immigration along the outskirts of Toronto is remarkable, and in some communities, over half of the residents are born outside Canada (for instance, in the suburban towns of Brampton and Richmond Hill). The celebratory emphasis on the aesthetic emblems of colonialism as a basis for landscape continuity, in this case, serves to remove others both materially and representationally from the landscape. Aesthetically effacing the presence and landscape histories of both people whose ancestors predate colonial settlement and perceived newcomers is an expression of power, and it is an expression of fear. It is fear rooted in xenophobia and racism that strives to preserve the imprint of whiteness in the name of ecology through supposedly altruistic environmental campaigns (Foster, 2009, 2010).

The concept of aesthetic justice can be mobilized to advance the environmental expression and experience of socio-cultural equity. First proposed by Monroe Beardsley (1973) in relation to fine arts, the concept emphasizes a distinction between aesthetic wealth in a community (its potentiality) and aesthetic welfare (its actualization) in service of aesthetic quality, which he describes as "the kind of pleasure or sense of satisfaction and fulfilment that comes from awareness of the way elements of experience interrelate in order to bring about the formation of complex unities that are marked by emergent regional qualities" (49). Beardsley positions these as distributive justice considerations and argues in favour of aesthetic policies that open up freedom of aesthetic expression through opportunities for engagement and support for the development of aesthetic capabilities within widely diverse groups. The argument is carried beyond distributive justice concerns by Mark Canuel (2006), who builds out the principle of aesthetic justice by challenging what he terms "beauty's problematic internal logic" that relies on a shared normative identity, as well as normative claims about what constitutes pleasure. The aesthetic justice perspective proposed by Hanna Matilla (2002) is especially persuasive as an approach to planning and design. Incorporating critical socio-political processes that reflect cultural practices that are formative of cities, Matilla's proposal works to validate alternative knowledge, histories, sensory preferences and signals of taste about urban social and ecological systems. This is an approach that could also allow space for disorderly nature to thrive.

In urban environments, aesthetic order is typically perceived in the form of tidiness as a reflection of care, a work ethic or a commitment to maintaining the attractiveness of one's community (Nassauer, 1995, 1997). In the Global North, this tends to align with conventions around scenic or picturesque features and is evident in the dominance of turf lawns as the most prominent horticultural investment. This aesthetic conformity leaves little space for ecological diversity in its many forms but particularly in the forms of what Saito (1998) calls "unscenic nature." Where ecological richness is unrecognized, where ecological assemblages are evaluated as simply messy and degraded, Saito argues, there is an aestheticized misunderstanding of biophysical processes that can gradually be remedied with enhanced public ecological literacy. Gandy (2012a) suggests that "unkempt" urban green spaces are aesthetically interpreted as symbols of waste, decline, impoverishment, neglect and political marginalization. However, he also observes that tolerance for these messy ecologies partly mirrors socio-economic differences, noting that they are more aesthetically acceptable among younger residents who are more educated and prosperous. He is certainly correct in terms of the trending desire for purportedly unmanicured park spaces that reflect a sanitized state of abandonment, such as New York City's celebrated High Line. In contrast, Saito's proposition builds off a broader legacy of appreciation for unkempt nature in cities that can be augmented through sustained ecological literacy. Aesthetic conceptions of space as *terrains vague*, for instance, present a compelling aesthetic alternative, a disruption in the reach of urbanized capitalism.

Terrain vague

The concept of *terrain vague* signifies a constellation of landscape expressions that are unregulated and indeterminate. Indeterminacy can relate to ownership, management ideals, boundaries, ecological functions, histories and futures. These are spaces that are typically considered to be empty or vacant, between distinct and legitimate planned stages of development. Correlated conceptions abound that invoke transgression and discovery, residuality and waste, ambivalence and void (see Foster, 2014). But what unifies them is an emphasis on refuge, collective tactics, lack of surveillance and peripherality to mainstream urban experiences.

Terrains vague are spaces that are primarily shaped by natural processes such as nutrient cycles, energy transfers and migration routes, where former land uses have been exhausted, divested, determined redundant or simply abandoned (Foster, 2014). As a result, they are spaces of prospects and possibilities, of fecund imagination. The term was coined by Spanish architect and philosopher Ignasi de Solà-Morales (1996) to describe the "non-spaces" that fall outside the margins of conventional urban form. Solà-Morales explains that *terrains vague* are "territorial indications of strangeness itself, and the aesthetic and ethical problems that they pose embrace the problematics of contemporary social life" (122). Popular examples of this landscape archetype include soggy riparian banks, old cemeteries, unkempt fields and overgrown industrial sites. They are spaces where decay and fertility intermingle, where crumbling buildings and infrastructure give way to vibrant new life forms and possibilities. They are messy, untended spaces, often perceived as defiled, with uncertain relationships to circuits of capital and wealth accumulation. As locations that have been conceptually, logistically and administratively demoted from economic growth nodes to wastelands, and they are places where novel ecosystems thrive.

The disconnection of *terrains vague* from the dominant logic of urban development is what makes them socio-ecologically notable. Since these spaces are not authored by particular designers or planners, they are not the subject of conventional agendas to beautify, control or surveil, and they do not play to popular Western greenspace signifiers of moral respectability. Nor do they correspond with landscape prototypes inviting leisure, such as athletic fields or hiking trails. As Lizet (2010) notes, they are spaces that may be read in complex ways, as exogenous yet indigenous, forbidden yet available and composed of material and symbolic waste. Plants and animals populating *terrains vague* are volunteers, finding their way by means of the unmanaged processes of species invasion. Colonizing the surfaces and structural faults of buildings and infrastructure, exploiting opportunities for undisturbed shelter and sustenance, organisms find their own habitat niches, unassisted by human hands. From the perspective of generalist species, these are ideal urban ranges. They are self-sustaining spaces, in that they thrive in the absence of human intervention. Yet amid urban settings, these spaces also provide unique opportunities to take advantage of contiguous resources, such as garbage bins, warm air vents, shelter and pooled water.

As irregular spaces in urban settings, *terrains vague* offer an aesthetic and ecological freedom that grants socio-cultural opportunities, especially for those who are marginalized from mainstream city life. Focusing on the ability to occupy and transform environments in ways unimaginable in conventional public open space, Anna Jorgensen (2012) portrays the experience for some people as "a highly psychologically liberating experience in which the individual is free to be whatever they want to be: whether that be meditative, playful, sexually active, or whatever they are able to imagine" (8). Because they are less regulated, *terrains vague* are places where bodies that are unwelcome elsewhere may find refuge and where alternate forms of urban engagement and inhabitation are possible. Thanks in large part to their status as defiled and unappealing to the urban majority, changes tend to be ignored. When changes are noticed, they tend to be accepted as part of the transitional character of the space, provoking only a mild reaction. For the most part, concern is dimmed by assumption that such space awaits its next legitimate use, even if potential future use remains unknown. Thus, the range of what is possible expands in these areas.

From an environmental justice perspective, *terrains vague* offer much to celebrate. These spaces can enhance access and contact with nature, especially for people who feel out of place in conventional parks and greenspaces or who prefer less manicured and regulated surroundings. They express different landscape values from the mainstream, paying no heed to dominant ideals, histories or affiliations. As described by Krystallia Kamvasinou (2006), they are multi-sensory "alternative public space" (257), responding to needs and desires disregarded in the rest of the city. Reflecting on the fixation on anti-social behaviours in the planning and management of urban parks and open spaces, ranging from legal ordinances to subtle design interventions, Catherine Ward Thompson (2012) observes a common bias against teenagers and young people, noting that

> often, unacceptable activities reflect the behaviour of older teenagers trying to establish their self-identity and a desire for territory of their own, which conflicts with notions of ownership, control and responsibility expressed by managers and other persons in authority, or by the community as a whole.
>
> *(51)*

Wastelands, derelict sites and abandoned gaps provide the urban wildscapes that are vital to childhood and adolescence, especially for marginalized youth. As she explains, "these flexible, 'loose-fit' places can often provide important places of escape for people with troubled childhoods, as well as for age groups of social or ethnic groups not welcome in conventional, well-supervised parks" (54). Alternative public spaces may provide relief from surveillance and other stressors, but they also offer opportunities for pleasure that diverge from the mainstream. Exploring the interconnections between industrial ruins and play (including destructive, hedonistic, artistic, adventurous and expressive forms of play), Edensor et al. (2012) explain that

> such spaces may be sought precisely because they confound familiar forms of comfort and mundane sensual experience. The transformed materiality of industrial space, its decay and the distribution of objects and less distinguishable matter, provide a realm in which sensual experience and performance is cajoled into unfamiliar enactions that coerce encounters with unfamiliar things, and encourage playful performance. . . . There are few consequences for engaging with matter or space in ways that transgress these norms, and the absence of surveillance provides an opportunity to do so with little chance for such engagements to be apprehended.
>
> *(67)*

An apposite sub-category of *terrains vague* that is resolutely urban is *délaissés urbains*. Like *terrains vague*, but typically smaller in scale, they are abandoned and untended, evolving quickly through seasons of neglect into rich habitats. Gilles Clément (2004) distinguishes these as ruptures in the urban environment that do not maintain clear functional relationships with their surroundings. These spaces are typically devoid of official usage, existing in a prolonged transitional state and vegetating spontaneously to support a great deal of biodiversity. They also offer important human benefits. In addition to contact with nature, they promote relaxation through physical activity, contemplation and respite from urban stressors. In this sense, *délaissés urbains* can furnish notable cultural services and contribute to a sense of wellbeing. Moreover, since they are less socially controlled, *délaissés urbains* can encompass more diverse spatial usages and practices than structured urban gardens and parks or formal open spaces. They can accommodate usages that are prohibited or less welcome elsewhere, provide open space for gathering and offer respite and refuge for those in need.

In a study of ecological attributes and appreciation of *délaissés urbains*, Brun et al. (2018) find that human interpretations of these spaces are complex and are strongly linked to the successional stage of vegetation. Appreciation is highest during the intermediate state, when *délaissés urbains* are considered to be most "natural." With too little vegetation, they are mere unattractive indications of blight and present as ecological disservices. Too much dense vegetation creates perceived barriers to human access and enjoyment. Overall, the study finds that people like *délaissés urbains* if they can be active within them. The transitional character of such space renders them difficult for many to appreciate in their own right, as ecologically vibrant in the absence of order and formal human codes of contact. Moreover, the study finds that *délaissés urbains* are less appreciated when they signal local problems such as vandalism, unemployment and homelessness. Rupprecht and Byrne (2014) identify a gradation of appreciation of *délaissés urbains* based on the intensity of surrounding urbanization, where they are more highly appreciated in dense urban milieus and less so in semi- or peri-urban settings. It appears that much of their appeal lies in their status as a counterpoint to built infrastructure and managed greenspaces with prescribed uses.

The aesthetic dimensions of *terrains vague* and *délaissés urbains* are profound, particularly in terms of ecological messiness. Since *terrains vague* are discharged from formal cultivation and management regimes, they are sometimes perceived as overgrown and weed-filled. This does not bother everyone, and messiness is also discerned in distinct manners. Lizet (2010) attributes their appreciation directly to the aesthetic qualities that they impart, with more vegetation contributing to a higher valuation than spaces cleared of greenery. Messiness presents the ecological foundation of Higgs' (2003) conception of wild design, where the prerequisites of sovereign ecosystems are prioritized through deliberate planning and design decisions that enable these to flourish unassisted. Allowing natural processes to prosper in this manner certainly means withholding overwrought human interventions, but it also means understanding what is needed for ecosystems to thrive in their own right, without constant tending or management, and ensuring that those needs are foregrounded. It is an inversion of conventional conceptions of landscape design as a set of outcomes and relies far more on unseen or imperceptible qualities that underly ecosystem wellbeing as constantly in flux. As unsightly after-effects of capital accumulation, these spaces have, at least temporarily, been released from the cycle of urbanization, which sets them out of sight from those with scenic and picturesque preoccupations. As a result, post-industrial spaces in which greenness manifests as *terrains vague* host robust natural succession processes through migration, breeding, seed dispersal, accumulation of soil biomass, hunting, sheltering, slow decomposition and water accretion. Free from dominant aesthetic coding, they are not expected to look or feel any particular way, and the range of possible engagements is vast.

Conclusions

Understanding the complexities of post-industrial urban greenspaces demands not only a commitment to ecological literacy but also an awareness of the forces of capitalism that have structured and continue to structure the conditions within which they exist. As novel ecologies, these are dynamic sites where natural succession is less impeded by the burdens of human management. They are suffused with the struggles of environmental justice, and they are spaces where environmental aesthetics are always fully activated. But they also stir important questions that are not easily answered. What is the responsibility to render history visible, especially where that history is unsavoury or harmful? How should the scars of industrialization be honoured, including those that cause destruction and environmental peril? What are the ethics of creating contaminated greenspaces that attract wildlife and intensify exposure to unsafe contaminants? How can urban ecology infuse planning strategies by and for marginalized communities? How can post-industrial greenspaces be planned and designed to respect unique attributes and possibilities? And when should we simply let these spaces evolve on their own terms?

These conceptual links and questions lay the groundwork for the next three chapters, where expansive post-industrial greenspaces in Paris, Milwaukee and Toronto are explored in detail. In Milwaukee, we find vast greenspace in what was once the "machine shop of the world," driven by a commitment to environmental justice and reinvestment in the city's core. In Paris, we find a 32-km-long continuous greenspace lacing through the "capital of modernity," mostly left fallow and wild in the wake of deindustrialization. In Toronto, we find a world-class bird refuge and verdant urban wilderness comingling with heavy machinery on a 5-km-long dump jutting into Lake Ontario. Each of these greenspaces has evolved in unique ways, suggesting that the range of possible futures is unbounded. There is no received wisdom or set of best practices concerning how these post-industrial urban greenspaces should evolve, and each heads along a unique trajectory towards urban sustainability.

Note

1 Noting that interpretations vary across Indigenous communities, the Minnesota Two-Spirit Society (2014) describes two-spirited people as "Indigenous North Americans who fulfill one of many mixed gender roles found traditionally among many Native Americans and Canadian First Nations Indigenous groups. The mixed gender roles encompassed by the term, historically included wearing the clothing and performing work associated with both men and women."

Bibliography

Agyeman, J., Bullard, R. D., & Evans, B. (2003). *Just sustainabilities: Development in an unequal world*. The MIT Press.

Akese, G. A., & Little, P. C. (2018). Electronic waste and the environmental justice challenge in Agbogbloshie. *Environmental Justice, 11*(2), 77–83.

Amuzu, D. (2018). Environmental injustice of informal E-waste recycling in Agbogbloshie-Accra: Urban political ecology perspective. *Local Environment, 23*(6), 603–618.

Anguelovski, I. (2014). *Neighborhood as refuge: Community reconstruction, place remaking, and environmental justice in the city*. The MIT Press.

Babcock, C. R. (1980, May 18). Chromosome harm found in love canal residents. *Washington Post*. www.washingtonpost.com/archive/politics/1980/05/18/chromosome-harm-found-in-love-canal-residents/f057f2dc-ba09-4c16-8287-926c7e2650ba/.

Beardsley, M. C. (1973). Aesthetic welfare, aesthetic justice, and educational policy. *Journal of Aesthetic Education, 7*(4), 49–61.

Blanc, N. (2012). Ethics and aesthetics of environmental engagement. In E. Brady & P. Phemister (Eds.), *Human-environment relations: Transformative values in theory and practice* (pp. 149–162). Springer.

Blum, E. D. (2008). *Love canal revisited: Race, class and gender in environmental activism.* University Press of Kansas.

Brady, E. (2003). *Aesthetics of the natural environment.* Edinburgh University Press.

Brotchner, M. (2014, February 14). Personal communication.

Brun, M., Vaseux, L., Martouzet, D., & Di Pietro, F. (2018). Usages et Représentations Des Délaissés Urbains, Supports de Services Écosystemiques Culturels En Ville. *Environment Urbain/Urban Environment, 11.*

Bullard, R. D. (2000). *Dumping in Dixie: Race, class, and environmental quality* (3rd ed.). Routledge & CRC Press.

Canuel, M. (2006). Doing justice in aesthetics. *Representations, 95*(1), 76–104. https://doi.org/10.1525/rep.2006.95.1.76.

Castree, N. (2000). Marxism and the production of nature. *Capital & Class, 24*(3), 5–36.

Center for Health, Environment & Justice. (2015). *Love canal FactPack* (FactPack). Center for Health, Environment & Justice.

Chapin, F. S., & Starfield, A. M. (1997). Time lags and novel ecosystems in response to transient climatic change in Arctic Alaska. *Climatic Change, 35,* 449–461.

Clement, G. (2004). *Manifeste Du Tiers Paysage.* Sujet/Objet.

Coulthard, G. S. (2014). Red skin, white masks: Rejecting the colonial politics of recognition. The University of Minnesota Press.

Dee, C. (2010). Form, utility, and the aesthetics of thrift in design education. *Landscape Journal, 29*(1), 21–35.

de Solà-Morales, I. D. (1996). *Presente y Futuros. La Arquitectura En Las Ciudades.* Collegi Oficial d'Arquitectes de Catalunya/Centre de Cultura Contemporània.

Dillon, L. (2014). Race, waste, and space: Brownfield redevelopment and environmental justice at the hunters point shipyard. *Antipode, 46*(5), 1205–1221.

Dillon, L., & Sze, J. (2016). Police power and particulate matters: Environmental justice and the spatialities in in/securities in U.S. cities. *English Language Notes, 54*(2), 13–23.

Edensor, T., Evans, B., Holloway, J., Milington, S., & Binnie, J. (2012). Playing in industrial ruins: Interrogating teleological understandings of play in spaces of material alterity and low surveillance. In A. Jorgensen & R. Keenan (Eds.), *Urban wildscapes* (pp. 65–79). Routledge.

Finding Flowers. (2021, February 2). Food and gardens as remediation – with T'uy't'tanat-Cease Wyss, Aanne Riley and Joce Two Crows Trembla. Presented at the Miijim: Food as Relations, Toronto.

Forman, R. T. T. (2016). Urban ecology principles: Are urban ecology and natural area ecology really different? *Landscape Ecology, 31,* 1653–1662.

Foster, J. (2009). Environmental aesthetics, ecological action and social justice. In L. Bondi, L. Cameron, J. Davidson, & M. Smith (Eds.), *Emotion, place and culture* (pp. 97–114). Ashgate Press.

Foster, J. (2010). Landscape continuity: Ecology, power and social order in environmental planning. *Planning Theory and Practice, 11*(2), 167–186.

Foster, J. (2014). Hiding in plain view: Vacancy and prospect in Paris' Petite Ceinture. *Cities, 40*(B), 124–132.

Foucault, M. (1973). *The order of things.* Vintage Press.

Foucault, M. (1978). *The history of sexuality: An introduction, volume 1* (R. Hurley, Trans.). Vintage Press.

Gadamer, H.-G. (1989). *Truth and method* (J. Weinsheimer & D. G. Marshall, Trans.). Crossroad.

Gandy, M. (2004). Rethinking urban metabolism: Water, space and the modern city. *City, 8*(3), 363–379.

Gandy, M. (2012a). Entropy by design: Gilles Clément, Parc Henri Matisse and the limits to avant-garde urbanism. *International Journal of Urban and Regional Research*, *37*(1), 259–278.

Gandy, M. (2012b). Queer ecology: Nature, sexuality, and heterotopic alliances. *Environment and Planning D: Society and Space*, *30*(4), 727–747.

Gobster, P. H. (2012). Appreciating urban wildscapes: Towards a natural history of unnatural places. In A. Jorgensen & R. Keenan (Eds.), *Urban wildscapes* (pp. 33–48). Routledge.

González, A. (2019). Racial capitalism and nature. *American Quarterly*, *71*(4), 1155–1167.

Gregson, N., & Crang, M. (2010). Materiality and waste: Inorganic vitality in a networked world. *Environment and Planning A: Economy and Space*, *42*(5), 1026–1032.

Haraway, D. J. (2016). *Staying with the trouble: Making Kin in the Chthulucene*. Duke University Press.

Harvey, D. (1996). *Justice, nature and the geography of difference*. Blackwell.

Harvey, D. (2008). The right to the city. *New Left Review*, *53*. https://newleftreview.org/issues/ii53/articles/david-harvey-the-right-to-the-city.

Hay, A. M. (2009). Recipe for disaster: Motherhood and citizenship at love canal. *Journal of Women's History*, *21*(1), 111–134.

Heynen, N., Kaika, M., & Swyngedouw, E. (Eds.). (2006). *In the nature of cities: Urban political ecology and the politics of urban metabolism*. Routledge.

Higgs, E. (2003). *Nature by design: People, natural process, and ecological restoration*. The MIT Press.

Higgs, E. (2017). Novel and designed ecosystems. *Restoration Ecology*, *25*(1), 8–13.

Hobbs, R. J., Arico, S., Aronson, J., Baron, J. S., Bridgewater, P., Cramer, V. A., Epstein, P. R., Ewel, J. J., Klink, C. A., Lugo, A. E., Norton, D., Ojima, D., Richardson, D. M., Sanderson, E. W., Valladares, F., Vilà, M., Zamora, R., and Zobel, M. (2006). Novel ecosystems: Theoretical and management aspects of the new ecological world order. *Global Ecology and Biogeography*, *15*(1), 1–7.

Hobbs, R. J., Higgs, E., Hall, C. M., Bridgewater, P., Stuart Chapin, F., Ellis, E. C., Ewel, J. J., Hallet, L. M., Harris, J., Hulvey, K. B., Jackson, S. T., Kennedy, P. L., Kueffer, C., Lach, L., Lantz, T. C., Lugo, A. E., Mascaro, J., Murphy, S. D., Nelson, C. R., Perring, M. P., Richardson, D. M., Seastedt, T. R., Standish, R., Starzomski, B. M., Suding, K. N., Tognetti, P. M., Yakob, L. and Yung, L. (2014). Managing the whole landscape: Historical, hybrid, and novel ecosystems. *Frontiers in Ecology and the Environment*, *12*(10), 557–564.

Hood, W. (2020). Black landscapes matter. In W. Hood & G. Mitchell Tada (Eds.), *Black landscapes matter* (pp. 1–8). University of Virginia Press.

Hornik, K., Cutts, B., & Greenlee, A. (2016). Community theories of change: Linking environmental justice to stakeholder perceptions in Milwaukee (WI, USA). *International Journal of Environmental Research and Public Health*, *13*(10).

Johnson, A. (2011). How to queer ecology: One goose at a time. *Orion Magazine*. https://orionmagazine.org/article/how-to-queer-ecology-once-goose-at-a-time/.

Jorgensen, A. (2012). Introduction. In A. Jorgensen & R. Keenan (Eds.), *Urban wildscapes* (pp. 1–14). Routledge.

Kaika, M. (2012). *City of flows: Modernity, nature, and the city* (pp. 1–257). Taylor and Francis.

Kamvasinou, K. (2006). Vague parks: The politics of late twentieth-century urban landscapes. *Arq*, *10*(3/4), 255–262.

Kattan, G. H., Aronson, J., & Murcia, C. (2016). Does the novel ecosystem concept provide a framework for practical application and a path forward? A reply to Miller and Beestelmeyer. *Restoration Ecology*, *24*(6), 714–716.

Kowarik, I., & von deer Lippe, M. (2018). Plant population success across urban ecosystems: A framework to inform biodiversity conservation in cities. *Journal of Applied Ecology*, *55*(5), 2354–2361.

Lefebvre, H. (1968). *Le Droit a La Ville*. Anthropos.

Liboiron, M. (2021). *Pollution is colonialism*. Duke University Press.

Lizet, B. (2010). Du Terrain Vague à La Friche Paysagée: Le Square Juliette-Dodu, Paris, X. *Ethnologie Francaise*, *40*(4), 597–604.

Loyd, J., & Bonds, A. (2018). Where do Black lives matter? Race, stigma, and place in Milwaukee, Wisconsin. *The Sociological Review*, *66*(4), 898–918.

Lupino-Smith, E. (2018, March 29). Morality cuts: Uncovering queer urban ecologies. *Guts*. http://gutsmagazine.ca/morality-cuts/.

MacGregor-Fors, I. (2011). Misconceptions or misunderstandings? On the standardization of basic terms and definitions in urban ecology. *Landscape and Urban Planning*, *100*(4), 347–349.

Marris, E. (2010). The new normal. *Conservation Magazine*, *11*(2). www.conservationmagazine. org/2010/06/the-new-normal/.

Mattila, H. (2002). Aesthetic justice and urban planning: Who ought to have the right to design Cities? *GeoJournal*, *58*, 131–138.

McGee, J. A., & Greiner, P. T. (2020, June 5). Racial justice is climate justice: Racial capitalism and the fossil economy. *Hampton Institute*. www.hamptonthink.org/read/racial-justice-is-climate-justice-racial-capitalism-and-the-fossil-economy.

McGregor, D., Whitaker, S., & Sritharan, M. (2020). Indigenous environmental justice and sustainability. *Current Opinion in Environmental Sustainability, Indigenous Conceptualizations of 'Sustainability*, *43*, 35–40.

McGurty, E. M. (2007). Transforming environmentalism: Warren County, PCBS, and the origins of environmental justice. New Brunswick, NJ: Rutgers University Press.

McIntyre, N. E., Knowles-Yánez, K., & Hope, D. (2000). Urban ecology as an interdisciplinary field: Differences in the use of 'urban' between social and natural sciences. *Urban Ecosystems*, *4*, 5–24.

McKittrick, K. (2006). *Demonic grounds: Black women and the cartographies of struggle*. University of Minnesota Press.

McKittrick, K. (2021). *Dear science and other stories*. Duke University Press.

McMillen, H. L., Campbell, L. K., Svendsen, E. S., Kealiikanakaoleohaililani, K., Francisco, K. S., & Giardina, C. P. (2020). Biocultural stewardship, indigenous and local ecological knowledge, and the urban crucible. *Ecology and Society*, *25*(9).

Meyerson, H. (2015, October 12). How the Bronx came back (but didn't bring everyone along). *The American Prospect*. https://prospect.org/api/content/035546a1-9476-5270-bf69-4987a86d494f/.

Miller, J. R., & Bestelmeyer, B. T. (2016). What's wrong with novel ecosystems, really? *Restoration Ecology*, *24*(5), 577–582.

Millington, N., & Lawhon, M. (2019). Geographies of waste: Conceptual vectors from the global south. *Progress in Human Geography*, *43*(6), 1044–1063.

MN Two-Spirit Society. (2014). *Walking in two worlds: Understanding the two-spirit and LGBTQ community*. http://www.tribal-institute.org/2014/INCTwo-SpiritBooklet.pdf.

Moore, S. A. (2012). Garbage matters: Concepts in new geographies of waste. *Progress in Human Geography*, *36*(6), 780–799.

Mortimer-Sandilands, C., & Erikson, B. (Eds.). (2010). *Queer ecologies: Sex, nature, politics, desire*. Indiana University Press.

Murcia, C., Aronson, J., Kattan, G. H., Moreno-Mateos, D., Dixon, K., & Simberloff, D. (2014). A critique of the 'novel ecosystem' concept. *Trends in Ecology and Evolution*, *29*(10), 548–553.

Muskrat Magazine. (2019, June 12). Indigenous garden removed from Humber River Banks by City of Toronto workers. *Muskrat Magazine*. http://muskratmagazine.com/indigenous-garden-removed-from-humber-river-banks-by-city-of-toronto-workers/.

Nassauer, J. I. (1995). Messy ecosystems, orderly frames. In S. Swaffield (Ed.), *Theory in landscape architecture: A reader*. University of Pennsylvania Press.

Nassauer, J. I. (1997). Cultural sustainability: Aligning aesthetics and ecology. In J. I. Nassauer (Ed.) *Placing nature: Culture and landscape ecology*. Island Press.

National Inquiry into Missing and Murdered Indigenous Women and Girls (Canada), Buller, M., Audette, M., Eyolfson, B., & Robinson, Q. (2019). *Reclaiming power and place: The final report of the national inquiry into missing and murdered Indigenous women and girls*. www. mmiwg-ffada.ca/final-report/.

Navarro, J. (2014). Solarize-Ing native hip-hop: Native feminist land ethics and cultural resistance. *Decolonization: Indigeneity, Education & Society*, *3*(1).

Niemala, J. (2000). Is there a need for a theory of urban ecology? *Urban Ecosystems*, *3*(1), 57–65.

Noxolo, P. (2017). Decolonial theory in a time of the re-colonization of UK research. *Transactions of the Institute of British Geographers*, *42*, 342–344.

Patrick, D. (2014). The matter of displacement: A queer urban ecology of New York City's high line. *Social & Cultural Geography*, *15*(8), 920–941.

Pearce, F. (2015). *The new wild: Why invasive species will be nature's salvation*. Icon Books.

Pickett, S. T. A., & Cadenasso, M. L. (2017). How many principles of urban ecology are there? *Landscape Ecology*, *32*, 699–705.

Pulido, L. (2016). Flint, environmental racism, and racial capitalism. *Capitalism Nature Socialism*, *27*(3), 1–16.

Pulido, L. (2017). Geographies of race and ethnicity II: Environmental racism, racial capitalism and state-sanctioned violence. *Progress in Human Geography*, *41*(4), 524–533.

Purcell, M. (2013). Possible worlds: Henri Lefebvre and the right to the city. *Journal of Urban Affairs*, *36*(1), 141–154.

Ranganathan, M. (2016). Thinking with flint: Racial liberalism and the roots of an American water tragedy. *Capitalism Nature Socialism*, *27*(3), 17–33.

Ranganathan, M., & Bratman, E. (2021). From urban resilience to abolitionist climate justice in Washington, DC. *Antipode*, *53*(1), 115–137.

Rupprecht, C. D. D., & Byrne, J. A. (2014). Informal urban greenspace: A typology and trilingual systematic review of its role for urban residents and trends in the literature. *Urban Forestry & Urban Greening*, *13*(4), 597–611.

Saito, Y. (1998). The aesthetics of unscenic nature. *The Journal of Aesthetics and Art Criticism*, *56*(2), 102–111.

Saito, Y. (2008). *Everyday aesthetics*. Oxford University Press.

Schnabel, L. (2014). The question of subjectivity in three emerging feminist science studies frameworks: Feminist postcoloonial science studies, new feminist materialisms, and queer ecologies. *Women's Studies International Forum*, *44*(1), 10–16.

Shotwell, A. (2016). *Against purity: Living ethically in compromised times*. The University of Minnesota Press.

Simpson, L. B. (2017). *As we have always done: Indigenous freedom through radical resistance*. The University of Minnesota Press.

Simpson, M., & Bagelman, J. (2018). Decolonizing urban political ecologies: The production of nature in settler colonial cities. *Annals of the American Association of Geographers*, *108*(2), 558–568.

Smith, N. (1984). *Uneven development*. Blackwell.

Sullivan, R. (2010, September 12). The concrete jungle. *New York*. https://nymag.com/news/features/68087/.

Swyngedouw, E., Kaika,M., & Castro, J. E. (2002). Urban water: A political-ecology perspective. *Built Environment (1978–)*, *28*, 124–137.

Sze, J. (2006). *Noxious New York: The racial politics of urban health and environmental justice.* MIT Press.

Teelucksingh, C., Poland, B., Buse, C., & Hasdell, R. (2016). Environmental justice in the environmental non-governmental organization landscape of Toronto (Canada): Environmental justice in the Toronto ENGO landscape. *Canadian Geographer/Le Géographe Canadien, 60*(3), 381–393.

Thompson, C. W. (2012). Places to be wild in nature. In A. Jorgensen & R. Keenan (Eds.), *Urban wildscapes* (pp. 49–64). Routledge.

Till, J. (2005). The negotiation of hope. In P. Blundell-Jones, D. Petrescu, and J. Till (Eds.), *Architecture and participation* (pp. 25–44). Routledge.

Tomiak, J. (2017). Contesting the settler city: Indigenous self-determination, new urban reserves, and the neoliberalization of colonialism. *Antipode, 49*(4), 928–945.

Tuck, E., & Wayne Yang, K. (2012). Decolonization is not a metaphor. *Decolonization: Indigeneity, Education & Society, 1*(1), 1–40.

Walcott, R. (2021). *On property.* Biblioasis.

Whatmore, S. (2002). *Hybrid geographies: Natures, cultures, spaces.* SAGE.

3

THE MENOMONEE VALLEY

Milwaukee, USA

If you encounter somebody from Milwaukee, think twice before characterizing their city as part of the Rust Belt. They may correct you, asserting that Milwaukee never went rusty. It's true, to a degree, through a particular lens. Milwaukee does sit within the western end of what is conventionally considered prime Rust Belt, a swath of industrialized northeastern USA close to the Great Lakes, where industrial decline took root in the 1980s and continues today. However, thanks to a diversified manufacturing base, the city was not entirely ensnared by the socio-economic decline that typifies the broad regional experiences of disinvestment, job loss, poverty, forfeiture and abandonment of factories and homes. Yes, Milwaukee was hit hard by a shift to overseas manufacturing and automation beginning in the 1980s. Yes, there was a severe loss of capital and manufacturing jobs (White et al., 1988; Levine, 2008). And yes, Milwaukee is fraught with socio-economic challenges such as health disparities (Greer et al., 2013; Holmes, 2019), inequities in education (Becker, 2015), harsh poverty (Desmond, 2016; Smeeding & Thornton, 2018; Levine, 2019) and mass incarceration of Black residents (Loyd & Bonds, 2018; Leichenger, 2014; Mock, 2015), amid severe racial segregation (Gurda, 2008; Frey, 2018; Denvir, 2011; Maternowski & Powers, 2017). But while the city's status as part of the Rust Belt may be questioned, its standing as a cornerstone of the currently industrialized Midwest remains intact.

Milwaukee's diversified manufacturing base has provided a strategic advantage not enjoyed by other Rust Belt cities that are typically dependent on single industries like automobile or steel manufacturing. Where single-industry cities such as Detroit and Pittsburgh spiralled into economic freefall through gradual deindustrialization, with the most racialized and poor communities vulnerable to the deepest damage, the impact was comparatively attenuated in Milwaukee. The city is grounded in varied industries, with breweries, machine shops, garment factories, slaughterhouses, motorcycle and train engine factories and tanneries thriving for

DOI: 10.4324/9781315106403-3

over a century. Thus, the shock and overall impact of a massive company such as Harley Davidson moving production offshore do not disturb the supply chain or employment network of, for instance, the city's dozens of breweries. By virtue of this comparatively more resilient urban economy endowed with a highly skilled workforce, Milwaukee has averted the deepest perils of the cycle of Rust Belt breakdown and has been afforded opportunities to explore new and creative means of civic improvement. The revitalization of the intensively industrialized Menomonee Valley is a case in point, where environmental justice strategies foreground job creation and economic revitalization for marginalized communities living in toxic locales.

Milwaukee is well known as a blue-collar, working-class factory town where manufacturing jobs have historically been held in high esteem. So, it is perhaps not surprising that the city would play to its strength by focusing economic development on manufacturing and re-industrialization, rather than tourism, service, high tech or the "creative class" economies that preoccupy many other North American urban planning agendas. What is surprising, however, is the means by which re-industrialization has been pursued. By insisting on sharply defined green standards and well-paid jobs, the city created space and incentives that have reversed the tide of deindustrialization and attracted an impressive range of manufacturing facilities, including global production headquarters for renewable energy firms.

FIGURE 3.1 Menomonee Valley vista, 2019

Source: Image by J. Foster

This was accomplished against broad predictions that this vision and plan would fail. By 2016, the revitalization of the Menomonee Valley had garnered 125 new businesses and doubled total employment to 16,000 jobs (Woodard 2016) while opening access to verdant greenspace for the surrounding working-class communities. This is why City of Milwaukee Director of Sustainability Eric Shambarger (2015) describes the Valley's revitalization as the national "gold standard" that has "raised the bar of what redevelopments could look like."

Alongside its reputation as a blue-collar town, Milwaukee is also well known as one of the most polluted cities in North America. In particular, soil and groundwater contamination were major concerns through the twentieth century and into the period of deindustrialization. Of the three major rivers running through the city, all of which are heavily industrialized and contaminated, by the early 1990s, the Menomonee River was easily the most contaminated, with high concentrations of lead, zinc, suspended solids and faecal coliform counts (EPA, 1979). These are the legacy of industrialization and impervious land cover. Once affectionately known locally as "the armpit of the city," the Menomonee Valley's reputation has been inverted by a combined strategy for job creation, ecological regeneration, community health promotion and Indigenous economic self-determination, producing a commitment to environmental justice that is remarkable in its comprehensive scope and impact.

Achievements in the Menomonee Valley are compound, multiplying the cumulative impact of the overall strategy for environmental justice. By creating family-supporting jobs hand-in-glove with physical access to a central portion of the city that has historically divided Milwaukee, and by linking such access to active mobility and alternatives to fossil fuel consumption and vehicle emissions, the redevelopment of the Menomonee Valley provides a cogent approach to urban post-industrial greenspace. The biophysical benefits of remediation are profound and have a direct impact on the health and wellbeing of nearby communities, and the approach in this case also integrates land reutilization, materials recycling, stormwater management, shoreline stabilization, enhancement of local biodiversity and creation of extensive wildlife habitat. As the early stages of the 1980s industrial collapse set in and regional transition into the Rust Belt caught momentum, few would have expected a city like Milwaukee to expand manufacturing jobs, clean its notoriously contaminated valley, create vast new greenspace and tackle persistent local health problems. Even fewer would have situated this as part of a broader strategy for Indigenous sovereignty that challenges extractive capitalism in other parts of the state.

The valley that divides

Regeneration of the Menomonee Valley presents a rousing exemplar of what's possible with a serious commitment to environmental justice. Thousands of jobs have materialized, green space has been created and quality of life has improved for the surrounding marginalized communities. But the story is not without contradictions as well, such as the location of a large-scale casino in an impoverished urban community, with gaming revenue channelled towards environmental justice gains far afield. And while city planners and the Menomonee Valley Partners (MVP) prioritized ensuring investments benefit the neighbouring communities through innovative and painstaking design guidelines and terms of reference for all contracts, it is unclear whether the employment commitments established 20 years ago remain localized.

The Menomonee Valley is the most heavily industrialized part of one of the most heavily industrialized cities in North America. A prominent historic signboard erected along the Hank Aaron State Trail that runs the length of the valley explains:

> In the early 1900s, Milwaukee was the "Machine Shop of the World" and the Menomonee Valley was its engine. Farm machinery, rail cars, electric motors and cranes were all made in the Valley. Clay became cream city bricks. Wheat was turned into flour, hogs became ham and barley became beer. Cattle were made into meat, leather and tallow (soap and candles) with no parts wasted.
>
> In the early 1900s, six companies hired nearly 75% of all African-American workers in Milwaukee: Plankinton Packing, Albert Trostel leather, Pfister-Vogel Tannery, Allis Chalmers, Falk Corporation and Milwaukee Solvay Coke and Gas Co. Half of these were located in the Menomonee Valley but only one remains today.

Today, the Menomonee Valley is a 1,200-acre (485-hectare) brownfield that is three miles (5 km) long and 0.6 miles (1 km) wide and divides the city's north and south sides. Persistent racially segregation along the Valley is rooted in the legacy of institutional redlining beginning in the 1930s, restricting home ownership for minority populations (Foltman & Jones, 2019), and has produced what is known as the most segregated city in the United States (Reeves & Rodrigue, 2016; Massey & Denton, 1998; Gurda, 2008; Richards & Mulvany, 2014). Racial inequities in Milwaukee are expressed through diverse phenomena, including housing patterns, uneven access to transportation, racialized unemployment, disparities in food access and rates of incarceration that are experienced in the low-income, predominantly Black neighbourhoods known as the Northside, which begin along the edge of the Valley (Pettygrove & Ghose, 2018).

The Menomonee Valley is Milwaukee's most prominent topographical feature, formed by glacial meltwater draining into Lake Michigan 10,000 years ago. Its once marshy floodplains were filled by early European settlers, beginning in the mid-1800s, and excavated for the pale yellow clay bricks that give Milwaukee the moniker Cream City. It also became a magnate for industrial operations. As more and more factories, abattoirs and production lines settled into the Valley, the by-products and waste of these operations built up like sedimentary layers along its expansive floor. Contaminants travelled along the baseflow of the river and through groundwater and were supplemented by industrial operations along the upper ridges of the Valley. In 1903, the Valley became the birthplace of Harley Davidson Motorcycles. By the 1980s, it hosted breweries, stockyards and meat packers, tanneries, heavy equipment manufacturing, steam and diesel engine factories, foundries and bulk commodity storage; 120 acres of rail yards laced the Valley floor and a shipping canal funnelled cargo in and out of Lake Michigan.

Employment in the Valley peaked in the 1920s at more than 50,000 jobs (City of Milwaukee, 1998) but tapered to fewer than 14,000 by the early 21st century (Peterangelo & Henken, 2014). Meanwhile, there have been important demographic shifts in the surrounding communities. Milwaukee is a majority–minority city (Dennis, 2018). According to 2021 US Census estimates, the two largest racial groups in Milwaukee are white (44.4%, 35.1% for not Hispanic or Latino white) and Black (38.7%). The city's Black population has remained steady over the past 25 years, but the white population shrunk from 45.8% since 2018. But during this same period, Milwaukee's Latino population has grown exponentially, and much of this has been localized in what is known as the city's South Side, adjacent to the Menomonee Valley, which had historically been populated by whites of Polish descent. Today, Milwaukee remains hypersegregated, and the city splits right along the Menomonee Valley. Matthew Desmond (2016) illustrates how

> The Menomonee River Valley cuts through the middle of the city and functions like its Mason-Dixon Line, dividing the predominantly black North Side from the predominantly white South Side. Milwaukeeans used to joke that the Sixteenth Street Viaduct, which stretches over the valley, was the longest bridge in the world because it connected Africa and Poland.
>
> *(33)*

The Northside of Milwaukee is predominantly Black, poor and heavily policed. Writing about one of the city's most easily recognizable Northside zip codes, Loyd and Bonds (2018) observe, "the zipcode 53206 has become a spatial shorthand for talking about race, violence, and poverty without talking about structural racism, capitalism, or the institutions of violence that sustain racial capitalism" (899). Racially restrictive housing covenants, as well as blockbusting and exclusionary zoning combine with investment in suburban communities, decades of deindustrialization and neglectful landlords to the concentrated Black residents in the Northside and produced poor-quality living conditions with few employment opportunities. Construction of a north–south interstate highway in the 1950s severed the community, and poverty intensified with industrial closures in the 1980s, followed by an economic recession in the 2000s (Daleiden, 2020). Meanwhile, racially skewed disciplinary actions in the Milwaukee Public Schools system have led to Black students being suspended at dramatically disproportionate rates for all grades from kindergarten through high school (Losen et al., 2015; Richards, 2015), and aggressive policing has led to elevated arrest rates on the Northside (Tchakirides, 2018).

FIGURE 3.2   Menomonee Valley, North Side, 2015

Source: Image by J. Foster

A 2016 study by Marc Levine demonstrates how "there has been an unmistakable 'Latinoisation' of Milwaukee over the past quarter century, in schools, labor markets, and the demographic composition of the city and the region" (6), with the proportion of the population more than tripling since 1990, representing all of the net population increase since 2000. Without Latino increase, the overall population would have shrunk. The study also found the lowest levels of Latino suburbanization in the country, owing to the city's historic patterns of segregation, and a cultural generation gap where a higher proportion of the city's youth is Latino and a higher proportion of the city's elderly is white. Rates of poverty for both the Black and Latino communities are extreme and spatially concentrated. Meanwhile, educational attainment within the Latino community is low but rising, with rapid "Latinoisation" of Milwaukee school enrolment rising from 8% to 25.3% of students between 1987 and 2016 and high school graduation rates surging alongside college admission rates. The 2021 US Census figures estimate the city's Latino population at 19%.

The Hmong community in Milwaukee has also grown significantly since 1980 when US Census figures noted 550 Hmong-identified residents. The 2010 census records 11,904, and numbers have grown rapidly since then. Most of the early Hmong residents in Milwaukee arrived as refugees, as a result of American disengagement from the war in Laos and Southeast Asia. In an environmental scan of

Milwaukee's Hmong community that draws primarily from interviews and story-telling circles, Chia Youyee Vang (2016) notes that they "often joined other disad-vantaged groups in deteriorating neighborhoods" (12). This scan also reveals that Hmong Milwaukeeans participate in a higher level of political and civic engage-ment than their socio-economic status would predict and at a higher rate than other ethnic minorities and disadvantaged groups. Milwaukee hosts the third larg-est Hmong community in the United States, and this is the largest Asian group in Wisconsin (Pabst, 2013). Since the vast majority are drawn to Milwaukee in order to live near extended family (Vang, 2016), it is not surprising that the edges of the Menomonee Valley have attracted a concentrated Hmong community. The com-munity overall is afflicted by high rates of poverty and health disparities (Smalko-ski et al., 2012). While there has been considerable advancement in reducing the rate of poverty, many in the community were already living precariously before the economic recession of the 2000s and lost businesses and homes to foreclosure (Pabst, 2013). Meanwhile, there have been impressive strides in educational attain-ment, reflected in the establishment of the Hmong American Peace Academy that supports the Hmong language and culture for over 1,000 students from primary through high school. In 2013, 87% of these students qualify for free or reduced lunch programs, based on family ability to meet basic needs (Pabst, 2013). Despite research confirming that, as Vang (2016) describes, "the Milwaukee Hmong com-munity remains largely invisible to the larger community" (10), this community is consistently identified as a key stakeholder group that invests in communal advancement and is credited with helping to build headway in the revitalization of the Menomonee Valley.

Valley redevelopment and a political groundswell

Against commonly held expectations, during a time of economic recession, the City of Milwaukee was able to nurture employment growth. Even as the plan took root, sceptics proliferated. By 1997, Valley employment had dwindled to 7,095 jobs (City of Milwaukee, 1998). Since then, however, over 5,000 family-supporting manufacturing jobs have been created in the Menomonee Valley, in addition to thousands of service jobs at the Potawatomi Casino and Hotel and the Milwaukee Brewers baseball stadium. This was achieved through visionary leadership within City Hall, a transition that suggests robust possibilities for environmental justice and the power of coalitions composed of unlikely collaborators in the creation of post-industrial urban greenspace. But visionary leadership is not enough, and the remarkable success of the Menomonee Valley must be credited to an atypical alli-ance that worked hard to coalesce and push for ground-breaking environmental justice strategies. This coalition is distinct from the conventional public–private partnerships that often form around large-scale urban conversions, and it brought strategic advantages that could not be easily replicated. Diverse and once unfamil-iar stakeholders worked collaboratively through the MVP to plan and steer revival without a set of "best practices" upon which to rely. The types of comprehensive ideals they envisioned required imagination, creativity and tenacity, in addition to dexterity as new challenges and opportunities arose. The Sixteenth Street Community Centre played a lead role, as did a variety of established industrial operations seeking to fortify their factories and invigorate their workforce. The Forest County Potawatomi Native American tribe also provided leadership from the outset, sparking momentum during the difficult early stages and investing extensively in the revitalization. And community resident groups sat at the table alongside the Department of Public Works, the Metropolitan Sewage District and urban planners.

Beginning in the 1970s, the City of Milwaukee composed various plans and visions for the Menomonee Valley, some elements of which were implemented such as road improvements, land acquisition, clearing a few abandoned factories and establishing municipal facilities (De Sousa, 2011b). But by universal measure, at this point, the Menomonee Valley was an absolute dump. Of the many colourful descriptors Milwaukeeans use to describe this stage in the Valley's progression, there is agreement that it was a heavily contaminated, wretched landscape that was scary and unsafe for humans. According to Melissa Cook (2015) of the Wisconsin Department of Natural Resources, diesel fuel in the rail yards had accumulated to a depth of 3 feet above the water table. Others describe it as "a decaying void in the center of the city" (De Sousa & Gramling, 2003) and replete with "generations of toxic geysers" (Gurda, 2021). Other early stakeholders and nearby residents note how broken glass and metal embed open spaces across the entire Valley. Dilapidated buildings were everywhere and the bridge spanning the Valley was unsound, with crumbling superstructure and parts visibly falling off. Sightlines from within the Valley were completely obscured by tall grasses and vegetation. Escaped animals from the operating stockyards ran wild. The Valley also functioned as a communal dump for anyone who wanted to dispose of undesired items, and that included carcasses from the stockyards and meat packing plants. Not surprisingly, a pungent and foul odour pervaded, which could be detected far into the surrounding communities. Methane gas permeated the air. It became a "no go" zone for all but those who had a compelling reason to travel there for the few remaining jobs.

In the late 1980s and early 1990s, efforts focused on building a few major non-industrial facilities to occupy cleared portions of the Valley. These functioned like islands of recreation and capital accumulation surrounded by despoliation. Notably, Marquette University expanded its athletic facilities, the Milwaukee Brewers' built a new baseball stadium and the Forest County Potawatomi Community built a bingo hall. These early attempts to reoccupy the Menomonee Valley helped focus attention on the possibility of reusing the space. But they were not part of a coherent landscape vision that foregrounded soil and water remediation, much less equity or justice. Rather, the Menomonee Valley was regarded as a wasteland where unwieldy or undesirable land uses could be located. As Cory Zetts (2015), Executive Director of MVP since its inception in 1999, explains "If you didn't know where to put it, you could just put it in the Valley." For instance, there

FIGURE 3.3   Miller Park baseball stadium, 2019

Source: Image by J. Foster

were several proposals for maximum- and medium-security prisons, all success-fully opposed by local residents, businesses and the potentially adjacent Milwau-kee Brewers (Wisconsin Department of Transportation, 1995; Woodward, 2016). Jeff Crawford (2019), Attorney General of the Forest County Potawatomi Com-munity, illustrates the unsavouriness by explaining how the Potawatomi initially acquired the site for a bingo hall in 1988 (which eventually became their highly profitable casino and hotel) as compensation for being removed from their tradi-tional territories:

> At the time, it was some of the most desolate land you could possibly imag-ine. In other words, a great place to put an Indian tribe. We were basically put in a dump.

The Valley was a depressing and perilous eyesore, and its future disposition was unclear. Would it be captured by expansive retail, wholesale and warehouse trade with unstable jobs? Perhaps, it would be dedicated to seasonal uses? Would it turn into an entertainment district with expensive new condominiums and office com-plexes? Would it become part of the city's park system? Or would it simply be left fallow, collecting the city's waste indefinitely? A few large proprietors moved in, but it seemed like change was stagnating.

Forest County Potawatomi: lighting the flames

The Potawatomi, as Algonquian people, always had a presence along the southern side of the Great Lakes, including Milwaukee. When European settlers began inhabiting the region fur trade was a primary point of interaction and negotiation. According to Crawford, coalitions kept both the American colonists and British in check. Things changed dramatically, however, in the early 1800s, after the Potawatomi aligned with the British during the War of 1812. When the British withdrew from the United States, the tribe was weakened and the federal government went aggressively after the Potawatomi. Reservations were created to contain the tribes that ceded their lands through treaties, the last of which was the Treaty of Chicago in 1833 that relinquished lands in Indiana and Illinois and moved the Potawatomi west of the Mississippi River to Iowa, Kansas and Oklahoma along what became known as the "Potawatomi Trail of Death" (McKee, 1939; Woodard, 2016). However, as Crawford explains, the Forest County Potawatomi as a whole refused to vacate their homelands. While some left, many also returned. But they were continuously pushed north as settlers occupied Wisconsin. Crawford describes how "We were basically wandering our home land. We were homeless. We were refugees on our own land." In the 1850s and 1860s, while federal and state troops were still attempting to forcibly remove Potawatomi people, the Forest County Potawatomi remained ostensibly hidden.

By 1913, the Forest County Potawatomi Community was officially recognized as one of the eight Potawatomi bands, the only one that remained in Wisconsin (Derks, 2014). Community members were allocated scattered plots of about 11,000 acres of land in the northeastern part of the state, which was not their traditional territory but was attained through provisions of the *Indian Homestead Act* and compensation from the Treaty of Chicago. In addition to the intergenerational effects of marginalization and dislocation from their traditional territories, many community members were damaged by the traumatic and degrading experiences of boarding school, summarized by Pember (2019) as "institutions created to destroy and vilify Native culture, language, family, and spirituality." They did not receive financial compensation for the 1833 land cession until 1981.

By 1988, Forest County Potawatomi lands attained "reserve" status, the same year that the national *Indian Gaming Regulatory Act* was passed as part of the political and legal fight for Native self-determination (Akee et al., 2015). The Forest County Potawatomi Community are a forest-based tribe, but as Crawford explains, they were living among second-growth trees in a very depressed timber industry. While physical isolation from settler populations may have helped the Potawatomi retain some cultural traditions, the community was economically impoverished. However, big changes came with high-stakes bingo, which could be offered on trust lands in Wisconsin.

In 1990, the Forest County Potawatomi took over a chronically underfunded 11-acre school campus on the destitute north edge of the Menomonee Valley to run as the Indian Community School that could serve urban Indigenous people.

They also applied to open a bingo hall alongside the school. Neighbours objected and blocked the bingo hall, but the state was still willing to approve it with an alternative 7.5 acres of trust land further south, right in the Menomonee Valley. Although he describes the area as a desolate dump, Jeff Crawford also describes the bingo hall deal as a unique opportunity for the Potawatomi to return to their traditional homelands:

> Historically, that was the convergence of three rivers. There were a lot of wetlands. It was the pharmacy of the Indian tribes that lived in the area. There were campsites all around the Menomonee Valley. That was your grocery store. You would fish, and then get your wild rice. Menomonee is an Algonquian word referring to wild rice. That would be where you get you food, medicine and supplies. That's why there's villages all around that area.

The Forest County Potawatomi saw gaming as a viable means to a secure economic future, a future that could rebuild the cultural legacy of their ancestors and bring environmental and social wellbeing to the community. Forestry and tourism may be options based on local resources for a remote northern Wisconsin community, but these were not going to generate the funds necessary to challenge economic marginalization and sponsor the types of socio-cultural regeneration that the Potawatomi yearned for. An urban casino, on the other hand, offered unparalleled funding opportunities to tackle serious health, education and environmental issues. So, in 1988, the Forest County Potawatomi erected a 50,000-square-feet high-stakes bingo hall in the middle of the Menomonee Valley, 360 km from their reserve lands in northern Wisconsin.

The Valley may have been located at the heart of a metropolitan centre, but it was still inaccessible even for local Milwaukee residents, and the setting was utterly unappealing for visitors. Neighbouring properties were a coal-fired power plant and a slaughterhouse. Taxis would not enter the Valley, and even those who ventured in by vehicle did so without clear roads, lighting or signage. As a strategic measure to help potential patrons navigate the surrounding open wasteland, two large torch flames were erected to guide visitors to the bingo hall. Wealthier patrons simply flew in by helicopter.

For the first ten years, Jeff Crawford maintains that the Forest County Potawatomi improved the bingo hall as much as possible and bought a few neighbouring parcels but were not able to make a meaningful impact on poverty for the Potawatomi people, which was their ultimate goal. As a minority shareholder (40% for the developer, 30% for the school and 30% for the tribe), revenue was limited. That's why in 1997 they bought out the contracts with partners to become sole owners, renegotiated their deal with the State to include slot machines and black jack tables and built a 120-million dollar expansion. This was a massive risk for the Forest County Potawatomi Community, a tribe whose membership numbered at 486 in 1990 and 531 in 2000 (North Central Wisconsin Regional Planning Commission, 2011).

Proximity to downtown is a huge asset for any casino, and this casino wasn't just proximate to Milwaukee; it was right in the very centre of the city. Yet, barriers to access severely impeded the casino's ability to channel a prosperous economic future for the Forest County Potawatomi Community. Leveraging shared revenue with the state, which was a requirement of the gaming agreements, proved fruitful. To this end, the Forest County Potawatomi Community lobbied for these funds to be re-invested in improvements to the Valley itself, specifically into constructing a roadway through the length of the Valley that could be used for the casino, the baseball park and all future land uses. If the Potawatomi Casino couldn't be in a prime location, they would enhance the location itself, and if they built a road, then people would come. The City of Milwaukee had redevelopment schemes on paper for the Menomonee Valley for decades, and as Crawford describes, the Forest County Potawatomi "took their old plans, shook off the dust, hired an engineering firm, and developed the preliminary plans for engineering a road that would connect the Valley." They paid $250,000 for the engineering study, which galvanized various groups to collaborate on road alignment and visioning the future possibilities for the Valley. This was a critical turning point not only for the Forest County Potawatomi Community's strategy for economic development in support of Indigenous wellbeing and self-determination but also for the entire Menomonee Valley and Milwaukee's manufacturing workforce.

Putting the Valley on the map

The construction of Canal Street was completed in 2001. It ran from the baseball stadium at the west end to the river mouth at the east end, where the newly constructed state-of-the-art 6th Street Viaduct replaced the century-old dilapidated bridge that had impeded flow between the city's north and south sides (Lovely, 2001). It was the culmination of a series of big gambles the Forest County Potawatomi had taken, and it paid off in dividends. Canal Street made the bingo hall and casino accessible and connected. In terms of transportation circuitry, it linked the heart of the Valley with a network of surrounding local and regional roadways, as well as nearby interstate and auxiliary interstate highways. And from a visual perspective, Canal Street introduced new and easily discernable connections that were evident from the surrounding communities and overpasses, with clear pathways into and through the Menomonee Valley. It put the casino onto the map by changing the map. It also meant that people could visit parts of their city they had never experienced or had not experienced in decades. And it brought stakeholders together who had never before collaborated.

The City's desire for Canal Street had been established through momentum sparked during Mayor John Norquist's term of office, beginning in 1988. He was a champion of the Menomonee Valley revitalization, described by many as a political leader willing to follow a vision and take chances. Melissa Cook traces his commitment back even further, to the time when he was a State Senator representing Milwaukee in the mid-1980s. Under his watch, the city conducted the 1998

Market Study, Engineering, and Land Use Plan for the Menomonee Valley, which served as a key planning document for revitalization. Due to concerns about stormwater and flooding, the Milwaukee Metropolitan Sewage District funded the initial study and became one of the strong initial partners. It reflected a great deal of public outreach (through workshops, interviews and surveys) to residents and businesses, as well as analysis of local demographics, markets, land uses and existing bio-physical conditions. The study endorsed redevelopment of the Valley as an eco-industrial park and identified manufacturing as its highest and best use. Key factors supporting this recommendation include the downtown location, proximity to the existing freeway network and the concentration of skilled labour in the vicinity. The study also revealed a strong desire for greenspace, for both recreational purposes and flood control, as well as enhanced access to the Valley and opportunities for active mobility routes (City of Milwaukee, 1998). It combined support for the existing industry with measures to attract new industry through a sustainability framework that eliminates land uses that degrade the environment. This gave clarity to stakeholders and potential businesses concerning the City's intentions for the Valley and struck alternate uses such as warehousing or commercial retail from the range of possibilities. In terms of implementation, the plan recommended a series of eight action agendas, beginning with the establishment of a public/private partnership to advance the land use plan. As a result, the MVP was formalized in 1999 as a non-profit organization with the mandate to guide and oversee the redevelopment of the Valley.

The MVP is a unique organization. It assembles a rotating board of directors of over 20 representatives from the municipality, local businesses and industries, health and social services, community advocates and resident groups. It was established before the construction of major developments such as the new baseball field, the Potawatomi Hotel and Casino and Canal Street. These early, large-scale developments, however, were not inspired by MVP. Rather, the MVP set out to form a comprehensive strategic plan for the rest of the Valley landscape. Its approach to revitalization is defined through four pillars that support "a thriving Valley with a well-balanced mix of industrial, recreational, and entertainment uses that strengthen Milwaukee." The economic pillar prioritizes positioning resilient manufacturing companies proximate to workers' homes. The ecological pillar focuses generally on sustainable development and environmental stewardship. A geographically oriented pillar concentrates on renewing ties with the surrounding neighbourhoods. And the fourth pillar broadly affirms equitable opportunities for all.

The MVP governance structure is organized around the board of directors and an advisory team, tasked with both advancing the vision and adhering to it themselves (De Sousa, 2011b). The MVP board of directors is composed of less than one-third of business representatives, about one-third of government entities and at least one-third of community representatives. Benji Timm (2008), a Project Manager with the City of Milwaukee, describes the MVP as "a very diverse and powerful board to move development forward." Melissa Cook describes it as a means of establishing "elaborate partnerships" that ensured buy-in for revitalization from the outset. The Forest County Potawatomi were involved from the organization's inception, and Jeff Crawford explains the organization's value for the tribe in terms of collaborative potential:

> It's been good for us and the City of Milwaukee. But it's been good in a different way for us, because it's really a modern-day coalition building that we have not experienced in probably seven generations. We could work with whites, Hispanics, African Americans, wealthy business people, people working in non-profits. For us to work with such diverse group, it just made us so much stronger internally. Because Indians know about politics. Believe me, we run governments. But it's an isolated politics. This is more of an inter-community politics that we had to learn.

As innovative as MVP may seem, establishing an organization to oversee the future of the Valley was only the first step. Developing a detailed plan that responded to such a lofty mandate not a straightforward undertaking. The challenge was substantial, and there were no tenable cases in other urban centres with which to consult and from which to draw best practices. In effect, this ample mission also served as an advantage in ensuring that the strategic planning could be comprehensive and responsive to local circumstances and preferences. As Cory Zetts (2015) explains, the organization was "broad enough in scope that we can throw a lot in." The MVP began with community consultation to identify the most pressing needs. In these crucial stages, where the revitalization mission was substantively defined through a grounded plan spanning approximately 1,200 acres, leadership came from the local Sixteenth Street Community Health Centre (SSCHC), which serves Milwaukee's Near South Side neighbourhood, particularly underserved and disenfranchised community members without health insurance.

Building the plan through community health, sustainability and living wages

The first Vice-President of MVP was Peter MacAvoy, who was Director of Environmental Health at the SSCHC. By this point, the health centre was in a largely Latino neighbourhood immersed in old industrial sites. Elevated lead levels (almost 40% among children) had sounded alarms about local sources of contamination and the effects on community health and wellbeing. Once the most contaminated sites were identified, confined and remediated, attention turned to the rest of the neighbourhood. Residents needed to live safely in the community, with healthy and unpolluted places of employment, learning and recreation. In 1997, SSCHC established a Department of Environmental Health, which McAvoy et al. (2004) describe as responsible for "achieving a healthy environment within its service area through restoring abandoned, environmentally contaminated industrial sites; attracting high-quality investment; and creating family-supporting jobs to increase the prosperity of the low-income families it serves." SSHCH pronounced the circumstances a public health crisis in the community, based on issues such as asthma, diabetes, and disproportionate unemployment due to the loss of "walk-to-work housing" with deindustrialization. The health centre was full of people with lived experience addressing the connections between health, local environment and quality jobs, and this propelled the revitalization work. It enabled critical feedback between residents who might otherwise be marginalized from conventional urban planning processes and those steering the redevelopment. Mobilizing the front-line public health connections proved essential to this particular approach to environmental justice.

It is unusual for a large-scale urban redevelopment project to be driven by a community-based health service provider. But where environmental justice is concerned, this is exactly the type of organization that could offer meaningful leadership. By foregrounding the social determinants of health, and by linking these unequivocally to the ecological attributes of the neighbourhood, the SSCHC was able to approach the lofty MVP vision with concrete, front-line knowledge and experience that was responsive to the needs of the low-income, racialized community in the vicinity. Building on a situated and refined understanding of the social networks that could be mobilized, the SSCHC had already established its Department of Environmental Health to incorporate environmental conditions into an expanded analysis and programming for health services. Although uncommon at this time, this comprehensive and location-based approach also meant that the SSCHC was addressing planning as a primary function of its ongoing operations. As Nancy Aten (2008), the Landscape Architect who developed the *Menomonee Valley Landscape Restoration Plan*, which defined the transition of the Valley's industrial wastelands into ecologically biodiverse habitat, remarked in 2008:

> They were really, in a lot of ways, the instigators of this redevelopment. They are a community health facility and so they have doctors, and walk-in clinics and dentists and sort of the whole health spectrum and they serve our neighbourhood to the South.

Like many of the organizations that have made serious advances towards environmental justice, SSCHC was not focused on a single issue, but rather took a multi-pronged approach that supported health in conjunction with poverty alleviation, education, justice, civic engagement and other core elements of community wellbeing. Appreciation for the intertwining of various issues is further reflected in the ways that those active in environmental justice in Milwaukee conceptualize the relationship between humans and their environment. Contrary to the claims of some urban political ecology writings, those active on the ground, in localized settings of everyday environmental justice work, have a sophisticated appreciation of the co-production of nature and culture. As Hornik et al. (2016) explain in their

exploration of conceptualization of water resources among those with lived experience of the production of justice and injustice in Milwaukee,

> The idea of a human-nature binary is depicted in numerous papers and posi-
> tioned as problematic for how people understand socio-ecological interac-
> tions. . . . We observed very little delineation between environmental and
> social factors – evidence that our stakeholders perceive these factors as inter-
> acting and influencing each other.
>
> *(7)*

Inspired by the 1998 *Market Study, Engineering, and Land Use Plan for the Menomonee Valley* and establishment of MVP, in 1999, the SSCHC launched a sustainable
design charrette for the Menomonee Valley in partnership with the University
of Wisconsin-Milwaukee. The design charrette led to the widely circulated 2000
publication of *A Vision for Smart Growth*, which, according to Peterangelo and
Henken (2014) "provided visual ideas of how individual parcels could be transformed and generated energy around the prospect of revitalizing the area as a
whole" (24). The report both strengthened and refined the vision of the Valley
as providing a green manufacturing future for Milwaukee. Following the success
of the design charrette, in 2002 SSCHC launched a national design competition
for a 140-acre former railyard parcel. At this point, the SSCHC also commenced
consultation towards the development of two sets of guidelines: directions for green
building and standards for family-sustaining wages.

2004 was a pivotal year for advancing Menomonee Valley revitalization from
ideals to actions. In addition to two key planning documents that link future
developments to environmental design and employment standards, one of the
Valley's largest and most polluted sites was cleaned up. The lands associated with
the 140-acre former Milwaukee Rail Yard housed rail infrastructure as well as
several factories. This was Milwaukee's most extensive brownfield remediation
project completed to date. Key concerns addressed through the project include
contaminated soil, old foundations, relic brick sewers and asbestos. In order to
limit the transfer of any remaining contaminants, the site was capped with excess
soil from nearby highway interchange construction. The clean-up produced a
100-acre business park, with Environmental Protection Agency (EPA)-approved
parcels ready for sale to potential new industrial manufacturers. It also produced
a 40-acre stormwater park, planted with native species to capture, filter and help
cleanse every drop of rain water from the business park through recreation fields,
open space and river connections. The 24-acre Three Bridges Park includes winding paved trails and bridges across the river, as well as raised community garden
planters and river access points for fishing or launching a boat, but is mostly a
self-organizing, wild urban meadow prairie. Given the dramatic urban ecological
transformations that this part of the city had experienced over the past century and
a half, restoration work embraced the landscape as a novel ecosystem, emphasizing
the existing relationships as they had evolved, not as they might be envisioned in

some pre-colonial imaginary. There were no efforts to rid the landscape of undesirable species, and the industrial heritage of the Valley is foregrounded as the baseline ecological condition through which nature is interpreted and celebrated. Remediation work creates self-sustaining habitat, without intensive management, and evolves rapidly. The restoration work focused primarily on creating the conditions for urban wilderness to thrive. Announcing the completion of the remediation project, Mayor Tom Barrett stated: "The vacant eyesore of the 1980's is gone and finally the renewal can begin" and "Milwaukee's most visible eyesore is now one of our most visible opportunities to attract jobs to this city" (City of Milwaukee, 2004). A hefty portion of the Valley had been transformed, presenting an appealing prospect for potential businesses, and it was time to release the preconditions for future proprietors.

The *Menomonee Valley Sustainability Design Guidelines* were disseminated in 2004. They are oriented towards investors, builders, project managers and companies seeking to locate in the Valley, providing guidance on "high performance building." The guidelines advise that they "help you get more return on the investments that you make in your building and your site, and help you meet your regulatory standards more efficiently." Although they are not mandated, adherence to the *Design Guidelines* effectively became a condition of development permit approval for any organizations interested in the Valley. Now that industrial manufacturing had been firmly established as the desired land use, alongside the provision of greenspace and recreation opportunities, the *Design Guidelines* would offer clear expectations concerning the re-establishment of industrial facilities. The guidelines were certainly ambitious for their time, addressing not only material and energy concerns but also worker health and the quality of workplace experiences.

Where the MVP remained responsible for the overall direction of the Valley's revitalization, the *Design Guidelines* direct developers about planning, design and construction matters at the site level. They provide clear guidance on adaptive reuse as the overall approach to site design, recognizing the river as the ecological context alongside industrial heritage, the natural landscape, existing building stock and landmarks. Building design is coupled with energy efficiency and promotes "a uniform and inviting sense of place for employees and customers," for instance, by means of daylighting techniques, building orientation towards Canal Street and screening noise and odours. The new construction incorporates a minimum of 5% on-site renewable energy generation (such as small wind, solar, and solar electric heating and cooling). Wherever feasible, closed-loop geothermal is advised. In terms of materials, the *Design Guidelines* set goals of 35% recycled building materials, 20% materials manufactured within a 500-mile radius and 25% US Forest Stewardship Council-certified wood-based materials. There are specifications for air barriers, coatings, sealing, adhesive carpet systems and restrictions on the use of urea-formaldehyde resins and chlorofluorocarbons. High-efficiency plumbing, cooling towers and replacement of leaking or lead laterals are stipulated. During the construction and demolition processes, at least 75% of waste materials must be salvaged, and erosion control plans must conform to the best practice standards.

Concerning indoor environments, the indoor air and acoustic quality must provide a healthy and productive work space, increase comfort and alertness, improve productivity and reduce absenteeism. The *Design Guidelines* include building operations and maintenance standards to ensure accordance with building performance targets, protect the health and welfare of workers, minimize the impact on the surrounding environment and ensure long-term landscape stewardship. Properties must be connected to a bioretention facility the MVP constructed as an inter-property regional stormwater treatment area. Any properties not connected to the bioretention facility must capture and treat all stormwater on site. Native species must be selected for 80% of site plantings, and landscaping must be oriented towards the minimization of pesticides, herbicides and fertilizers (which can only be organic). Deep-rooted grasses and vegetation should replace turf, and invasive species should be removed from within parcel boundaries. In terms of the regional transportation network, facilities are encouraged to incorporate pedestrian pathways and bike stations, showers and changing facilities for employees, post "no idling" regulations and eliminate winter salting by replacing the practice with steam infrastructure that melts ice and snow.

At the same time that the *Design Guidelines* were being composed, the MVP also established wage criteria for workers. These two sets of standards were conjoined as the minimum expectations for any new businesses that would become part of the revitalized Menomonee Valley. As noted, manufacturing jobs have historically

FIGURE 3.4   Menomonee Valley bioretention facility, 2013

Source: Image by J. Foster

been esteemed in Milwaukee, forming the backbone of the city's industrial economy. These jobs evaporated in the late twentieth century, tumbling from 104,451 (34.8%) in 1970 to 90,307 (31.8%) in 1980 and down to 60,991 (22.4%) by 1990 (City of Milwaukee, 1998). Blue-collar jobs had historically furnished a comfortable quality of life for workers, and they are jobs that maintained place of pride in the civic imagination. Couched with the goal of bringing back manufacturing jobs, which was determined through extensive community consultation by SSCHC, was the insistence that these are jobs for which employees are well remunerated. Quality employment opportunities were envisioned as the current that could enliven each of the four pillars of the MVP mandate. In terms of defining what constitutes appropriate remuneration, De Sousa (2011b) notes, "Milwaukee's Department of City Development, local businesses, and key stakeholders in the surrounding community did come to a general agreement that the area needed to be revitalized to provide 'family supporting' jobs" (2).

The goal of family-supporting jobs, however, did not go unchallenged by alternate interests, namely, those of existing proprietors of the lands in question. Corey Zetts explains how the vision emerged and was contested:

> In the very early beginning there was the proposal to just turn this into park space. But the residents were the ones who came out and said that parks are nice and we like parks but we really need jobs. That was a big part of the city's decision to keep land for manufacturing, because that was really what the skill set of the surrounding neighborhoods was and more likely to pay living wage jobs. There was a lot of litigation because the entity that owned the surrounding land wanted it to be developed as an entertainment district to support the stadium.

The family-sustaining target was clearly defined in a 2004 MVP report that focused specifically on the redevelopment of a stockyard, which set a job density target of 1.5 jobs per 1,000 square feet, at a minimum rate of $12/hour for full-time work and $8/hour for part-time work. The report endorsed employer-paid health care, benefits and opportunities for advancement, as well as a commitment to hiring neighbourhood residents (MVP, 2004). The report also affirmed that preference would be given to prospects that "have the highest potential for increasing the neighborhood's and the metro area's income." In 2005, the family-sustaining targets became formal policy governing any land sales by the City (Peterangelo & Henken, 2014), with the minimum wage target set at the MVP rate of $12 per hour, which was more than double the state's minimum wage at the time (De Sousa, 2011b).

Realizing the vision with new planning methods and techniques

The formidable work of Indigenous, health centre and community and resident groups was bolstered by municipal commitments that helped bind the revitalization planning and implementation. Although a visionary mayor may have cast the seeds of revitalization, dedicated municipal employees helped ensure that they would germinate and thrive through innovative municipal planning strategies. The context for municipal policy and planning in Milwaukee at large remained firmly neoliberal, a key feature of which centred on transforming so-called unproductive land through private–public partnerships, often with the effect of reproducing white-favouring and colonial spatial patterns and relationships that did not challenge the structural roots of racism, poverty or oppression of Indigenous people (Pettygrove & Ghose, 2018). In the case of the Menomonee Valley, Peterangelo and Henken (2014) summarize the perspective of "city leaders," who characterize their role as "creating the conditions needed to facilitate high-quality private sector investments by establishing and enforcing regulations, building and improving infrastructure, and supporting partnerships between public and private sector entities" (19). Such a generic description of the assignments and obligations, however, does not capture the creative manner with which Milwaukee planners approached the Menomonee Valley challenge and does not relay the ways that their choices also helped dilute neoliberal economic development practices. Bridging the vision, ideals and *Design Guidelines* with positive health, environmental and employment outcomes while enhancing community connectivity was a tall order that required novel planning tactics and a great deal of resolve. Planners had to think in innovative ways and hold their ground against the tide of late capitalist planning models that prioritize cheap labour, feeble environmental standards and shallow civic commitments. Furthermore, they had to convince potential businesses to invest in the Valley in the face of vocal naysayers and detractors who prophesized failure in attaining the plan's goals.

City planners were able to shepherd brownfield grants dedicated to cleaning up the most toxic portions of the Menomonee Valley. An estimated $200 million in public funds has been invested in the clean-up and revitalization (De Sousa, 2021), and the city planners were instrumental in steering the foundational clean-up work that enabled the rest of the Valley revitalization to progress. Among the first was a brownfield grant from the EPA to begin decontaminating the river valley, coupled with funding from the federal Department of Housing and Urban Development. There were no prototypes for this large-scale approach to deep contamination, and City planners had to invent their own methods and practices. As the City of Milwaukee Senior Environmental Project Coordinator Tory Kress (2008) explains, "We kind of lead. I think that the EPA looks to us a lot of times to see how we're doing things here, but we sort of took the reins and are still pushing ahead." Project Manager Benji Timm (2008) relates how they approached the work as a "voyage into experimentation" and describes his fruitless attempts to seek guidance from federal and state agencies, as well as brownfield planners in other large municipalities:

> I called them up and I said "hey we're, we're moving toward undertaking this, this larger project. Can you give me some examples of other similar-scale projects or other good ideas you've heard about in other cities?" And two of them responded back with, "well, we usually tell them to call Milwaukee."

Milwaukee Riverkeeper Cheryl Nenn (2008) clarifies that the City was on the vanguard of brownfield remediation in general and that "they've been pretty aggressive along the riverfronts in remediating contaminated sites." The City's innovation went beyond remediation of toxins though, for instance by converting a ship-turning basin on the Menomonee River into canoe access. Since the basin continuously collects floating trash, they had to invent a skimming and filtering system that could reach deep into the corners of the basin, which became a prototype for this otherwise stubborn problem.

In order to ensure observance of the *Sustainable Design Guidelines* that the Sixteenth Street Community Health Center had overseen, city planners had to develop new methods for large-scale projects. Preserving the working-class neighbourhoods around the Valley and directing the economic benefits of the development work itself towards these residents required the creation of new practices and protocols. Nancy Aten (2008) explains how planners divested from corporate developers by breaking up contracts, so large construction holding companies would not acquire a single overarching contract for the bulk of the redevelopment work. The redevelopment work was divided into scores of little contracts that could support small businesses, especially minority businesses. The City developed a designation called Emerging Business Enterprises (EBE) for local, small operations led by minority and disadvantaged contractors and reserved 41% of the contracts for EBE-qualified outfits. The City conducted training sessions for small businesses on matters like how to bid on a contract, how to get bonded, how to get liability insurance and what to do in order to become a sub-contractor. Small projects such as constructing boardwalks, propagating aquatic plants or building picnic tables from the former stockyard pens were separated and offered through local bidding processes – a direct affront to the conventional mega-build corporate bidding processes that bundle all aspects of the project through a single large contract.

Once the remediation work was completed and the EPA had approved the land for new businesses, the City agreed to attract manufacturers with family-supporting jobs by expediting municipal and state permitting approval processes. The City offered to assist new businesses in attaining the *Sustainable Design Guidelines* performance criteria. And once the Forest County Potawatomi investments in Canal Street were complete, the City upgraded all of the surrounding infrastructures by improving on and offramp access, lighting, sewage and stormwater facilities and connecting roadways and bridges.

When the Menomonee Valley Industrial Center was ready to be marketed to prospective businesses, some remained pessimistic about maintaining the plan's integrity. Cory Zetts (2015) of the MVP describes a high level of cynicism about the ability to actually attract new industry during an economic recession, especially according to the terms of the *Sustainable Design Guidelines*. She recalls the real estate brokerages "accused them of socialism and communism, predicted that the City will cave with the first warehouse that wants to move in, or people will get cancer from spending time working in the Valley." But it didn't take long for the first business to sign up in 2006, which was Palermo Villa Inc., one of the largest frozen pizza producers in the United States. By 2021, there were over 37 manufacturers,

FIGURE 3.5 Menomonee Valley passage from South Side community, across the river, to the new manufacturing facility, 2015

Source: Image by J. Foster

as well as automotive servicing facilities, construction and engineering firms and a growing number of breweries. A particular point of pride for many was the decision by Spanish wind turbine manufacturer Ingeteam to locate its North American headquarters right in the Valley. In addition to the expanded casino and ballpark, the Valley has become a destination for visitors who appreciate Milwaukee-specific attractions like the Harley Davidson Museum and Iron Horse Hotel, an upscale hotel for motorcyclists in an old warehouse.

The Urban Ecology Center (UEC) opened along the southern edge of the Valley in 2012, in an old tavern just uphill from Three Bridges Park. The UEC was a late partner in the Valley's revitalization, as described by Executive Director Ken Leinbach (2018): "Although the Urban Ecology Centre was only one of the dominos that helped in the redevelopment of the blighted Menomonee Valley, in this case, we were essentially the last domino to fall" (122). In partnership with MVP, they acquired $25 million to fund the Three Bridges Park, expand the Hank Aaron State Trail and construct a new centre. This was a new branch for the organization, expanding beyond the main facility in the city's Riverside West community. The main UEC goal is to advance ecological literacy, and this is realized through diverse ways of accessing and engaging with nature, through recreation opportunities, clubs, tool and equipment lending, camp and after-school programming, workshops, community kitchen options and providing space for

FIGURE 3.6   Urban Ecology Centre Young Scientist Club, 2015

Source: Image by J. Foster

people to connect and hang out together. The Menomonee work shifted the UEC mandate from environmental education to habitat creation and stewardship. It also provided an opportunity to connect with Milwaukee's often-overlooked Latino community. Today, the UEC functions like a gateway to the Valley for many local residents, particularly youth and seniors, with year-round programs that include the Nature Rangers, Young Scientists Club, bird monitoring groups, community gardens and fishing clubs. Reflecting on the impact of the UEC, Zetts (2015) observes:

> Even 5 or 6 years ago it would have seemed crazy that the UEC would have opened a branch here. Their model they look for is water access, some prairie and some forest. We had this forgotten river and that's about it. But with how quickly all of this parkland has developed, this really became a spot they were interested in. They've really become the front-door through which the neighborhood engages in the park.

Given its location in the Near South Side, the UEC seems to appeal primarily to residents south of the Valley. However, this does not mean that the Northside is disregarded. UEC has also opened a location further north in Washington Park, with community-responsive programming and similarly deep investments in ecological engagement on local terms.

Jobs, greenspace and Indigenous self-determination

There are many indicators that the Menomonee Valley revitalization has been a resounding success, supporting Shambarger's claim that it is the gold standard for revitalization. By 2015, the Menomonee Valley Industrial Centre was full (Zetts, 2015), with 14 new industrial facilities employing over 1,400 workers in family-supporting jobs. According to the 2017 *Menomonee Valley 2.0 Market Study*, much of the labour supply comes from immediately contiguous neighbourhoods, particularly directly south of the Valley. There are 60 acres of verdant public park, strict stormwater standards that enhance the river and habitat creation that combines native biodiversity with novel ecosystems. Existing connections to the Valley have been fortified, and new access points enable enjoyment of extensive trails and leisure opportunities.

Fulfilment of the 1998 goals led to the adoption of an updated comprehensive plan, *The Valley 2.0 Plan*. This updated plan focuses on new food and beverage manufacturing and public amenities, a corridor of design and décor businesses along the north edge of the Valley, expanding the industrial manufacturing district on the Near South Side and improving multi-modal connections between the Valley and adjacent communities (especially along the I-94 Freeway). The *Design Guidelines* were also updated in 2017 to reflect contemporary technological advances and clarify requirements for new buildings and renovations.

While improvements to the Menomonee Valley are striking, some of the biggest gains from revitalization are located hundreds of kilometres away, in northern Wisconsin, where gaming profits are concentrated for the benefit of the Forest County Potowatomi Community, in service of Indigenous ideals and priorities. In a video produced by Wisconsin Public Radio, Potawatomi elder Mike Alloway, Sr. affirms that "The impact of Indian gaming created a better life for a lot of tribal members." Notable improvements include cultural preservation, traditional language recovery, protection of land and water, education and health (Derks, 2014). This is consistent with the findings of a study by Akee et al. (2015) on the effect of the growth of Indian gaming on Native Americans living on or near reservations. The study finds that

> Gaming operations have had a far-reaching and transformative effect on American Indian reservations and their economies. Specifically, Indian gaming has allowed marked improvements in several important dimensions of reservation life. For the first time, some tribal governments have moved to fiscal independence. Native nations have invested gaming revenues in their economies and societies, often with dramatic effect.
>
> *(185–6)*

For the Forest County Potawatomi Community, the impacts are intense. Although Jeff Crawford affirms that for the first seven to ten years, money only trickled in, once the tribe acquired full control of the casino and expanded operations, they "got over the hump" and began funding social welfare programs. They built a health and wellness centre with their own money, without any grants or external funding, providing long overdue health care for elders and the community at large. The health centre now serves the surrounding five-county region and the entire northern part of the state. They also built a government centre to host administrative functions, the Forest County Potawatomi Tribal Court, family services and other communal needs. Recent high school graduation rates have been 100%, and college enrolment has risen. The tribe has invested in a food sovereignty strategy to provide culturally appropriate self-sufficiency for tribe members with the Bodwéwadmi Ktëgan (Potawatomi Farm, established in 2017), which includes a network of greenhouse tunnels, orchards, livestock, field crops, an aquaponics facility and a market store. Significantly, Crawford also emphasizes that the most critical dimension of this "resurgence of the tribe" is the learning traditions of cultural wisdom, language and gatherings, because for "a whole generation of elders, it's been beaten out of them by the boarding schools."

While environmental justice advances in Milwaukee may be impressive, new capital generated through the casino for the Forest County Potawatomi presented yet another extraordinary environmental justice opportunity: blocking a massive mine and expanding territorial sovereignty. The Crandon Mine, nestled amid disconnected land parcels of Forest County Potawatomi Community and other tribal lands, was a 1976 proposal by Exxon Corporation for a shaft mine to extract copper, zinc and other metallic sulphides from three sites adjacent to an Ojibwe Indigenous reservation. A coalition of four tribal groups (the Forest County Potawatomi, Sokaogon Chippewa Community, Menomonee and Mohican of Stockbridge-Munsee), a sportfishing club and environmental non-government groups (including the Sierra Club and Protectors of Wolf River) worked to oppose the mine. While these groups had until recent times struggled against one another for local resource access (Seppa, 1994), they banded together around deep concerns about treaty rights, land destruction, long-range water pollution and production and release of heavy metals such as mercury, lead, zinc, cadmium, arsenic and copper. There were also important concerns about the influx of outsiders, destruction of wild rice beds, disruption of hunting, fishing and gathering territories and dishonouring sacred burial sites. This formed what Zoltan Grossman (2017) calls an "unlikely alliance" that was grassroots, multicultural, rural-based, multigenerational and working-class.

The grassroots coalition had been fighting the mine for decades. But with revenue from the Potawatomi Hotel and Casino, they were able to amplify resistance with what Jeff Crawford describes as "busloads of lawyers, experts, economists and lobbyists just pounding them," to the point where it became financially unsustainable for the mining company to pursue the proposal. In 1998, the State Governor signed a mining moratorium, and in 2002, a Supreme Court decision enforced the rights of tribal nations to establish water and administer quality standards. This in turn led to the Sokaogon Chippewa Community developing EPA-approved water quality standards that the Environmental Protection Agency (2006) describes as "the highest level of antidegradation protection available under regulations for the water quality standards program." It also meant that no mines would ever be approved. Then, in 2003, the Forest County Potawatomi Community used casino proceeds to purchase 5,800 acres of mine lands for the Sokaogon Chippewa Community from Nicolet Minerals Inc. (which had been purchased from Canada's Rio Algon), using what Crawford describes as a "straw buyer." Subsequently, the 2003 *Fraser Institute Annual Investment Attractiveness Index* demoted the State of Wisconsin and evaluated it as the least attractive locale worldwide for the mining industry (Fredricksen, 2004). This was widely received among Indigenous groups and environmentalists as a dazzling victory and new chapter in the long history of resistance to extractive industries. While the achievement is tied to the Menomonee Valley, it does not directly benefit those living in the urban vicinity. It prioritizes Indigenous sovereignty, needs and aspirations, resonating with Tuck and Wayne's (2012) distinction between decolonial and broadly anti-oppressive approaches to justice. They clarify that

> decolonization in the settler colonial context must involve the repatriation of land simultaneous to the recognition of how land and relations to land have always already been differently understood and enacted; that is *all* of the land, and not just symbolically. This is precisely why decolonization is necessarily unsettling, especially across lines of solidarity.
>
> *(7, emphasis in original)*

The casino paved the way for revival of the Menomonee Valley, demonstrating the first glimmers of light (literally so, with the fire torches installed so that bingo patrons could actually find the hall) for inhabiting the valley in new ways. The Forest County Potawatomi Community invested significantly in the Valley and shot life into regeneration plans that had long gathered dust in City Hall. They took leadership in seeing the plan through, working collaboratively through the Menomonee Valley Partnership. The casino and hotel facility is among the largest employers in Milwaukee, if not the whole state, with over 2,700 employees (Levy, 2019; Johnson, 2020). Yet the Potawatomi Casino and Hotel does not abide by the "family supporting" pay standard (nor does the baseball stadium), with employees such as cleaners, housekeepers, attendants, cashiers and food workers earning well below the family-sustaining target rate of pay for manufacturing jobs. And the casino continues to grow, responding to the market trend for entertainment, with expansion into sports betting, a second tower and more performance space, while each tribe member typically receives over $70,000 annually (Spivak, 2017).

The success of the casino points to the socio-economic potential of degraded urban areas in comparison to ecologically unsullied areas. Crawford affirms that "Even though the Menomonee Valley was the armpit, literally the dump of the city, you still had better economic potential than a pristine area where there are hardly any people." For the Forest County Potawatomi, this meant the difference between continued impoverishment and economic stability, with resources to support health, learning and cultural revitalization and protect and reclaim vast tracts of land elsewhere. By 2000, over 90% of the tribe's budget came from gaming, and they contributed approximately $30 million yearly to the state, based on a rate of 6.5% of net wins prescribed in the gaming compact (Johnson, 2020).

Yet, the success of the casino also begs questions about the relationship with the neighbouring communities. Urban casinos in general tend to thrive where there is a struggling economy or no competing business to consume or dismantle, which also indicates a poorer clientele who are contributing to the casino revenue (Chadburn, 2017). This is consistent with the characteristics of the Potawatomi Casino and Hotel locale and neighbouring demographics. In a *New York Times* series about inequality called "The Great Divide," Barbara Dafoe Whitehead (2014) explains that

> Not surprisingly, the closer casinos come to where people live, the more likely people are to gamble at one. As casinos have spread into de-industrialized cities, dying resorts and gritty urban areas, the rate of gambling participation has grown among lower-income groups.

Research conducted by Welte et al. (2004) that examines the spatial relationships of gambling participation and pathology identifies neighbourhood characteristics that make particular casino clientele vulnerable, emphasizing that disadvantaged neighbourhoods are typically populated by disproportionately poor and disproportionately minority group residents. The authors explain that "the ecology of disadvantaged neighbourhoods promotes gambling pathology, and availability of gambling opportunities promotes gambling participation and pathology" (405). Combined with the tendency to offer lower-skilled jobs and rates of pay, it is not clear that urban casinos in and of themselves contribute to the promotion of equity and justice in cities such as Milwaukee. Still, by 2019, the casino had donated $19 million to local youth non-profit organizations through its Heart of Canal Street program (Levy, 2019), and its overall commitment to the revitalization of the Menomonee Valley is laudable. The particular case of the casino complicates the understanding of urban environmental justice by contrasting the sovereignty of the Forest County Potawatomi Community as a remotely located group that has been deeply oppressed for centuries and fought the state's largest mine with the wellbeing of poor, working-class and racialized communities in the casino's vicinity.

In all measures, Valley has been an outstanding success, except in terms of employment connections with surrounding communities. While residents in the vicinity do enjoy a less toxic living environment and improved amenities like parks, greenspace and an ecologically enriched river system, there are concerns that the newly created family-sustaining jobs are disproportionately occupied by people outside the community. As Zetts (2015) explains,

> As we were revisiting our mission, the first piece is creating jobs close to workers' homes. That's happened. There are thousands of new jobs in the

Valley. Polermo's is one example, where huge proportion of their workforce is from the surrounding region. But by-and-large all the new recruits are coming from the metro region. We still have these pockets of unemployment immediately surrounding. . . . In all the analysis we've done, on every other measure the Valley has been an outstanding success. But really connecting to the surrounding communities in terms of workforce is where we haven't made much progress.

A 2014 analysis of the ingredients of success in the Menomonee Valley revitalization finds that "Palermo's and the Potawatomi Hotel and Casino are the only Valley businesses that employ large numbers of residents of nearby neighborhoods" (Peterangelo & Henken, 2014, p. 5). There are several potential contributing factors inhibiting the rate of Menomonee Valley employment for local residents. One challenge is that training for trades programs that align with manufacturing jobs are concentrated at the Waukesha County Technical College, in the city's far suburbs over 30 km from the Menomonee Valley, where many companies recruit their employees through apprenticeship programs associated with the school's degrees, diplomas and certificates in manufacturing. The school is not accessible for downtown residents who do not have a car, childcare or the ability to travel long distances each day. Another challenge is the dearth of partnerships along the north side of the Valley. Key community-based partnerships like SSCHC and the Urban Ecology Centre are concentrated within Milwaukee's South Side, and the North Side, which is largely Black, does not have organizations that are actively and deeply connected to the Valley. This problem is compounded by physical access barriers for residents, especially the interstate highway that runs between the industrial portions of the Valley and the residential community along its ridge. Similar to the need for partnerships with community-based groups on the North Side, the need for accessible passageways similar to those on the South Side is unmistakable. Safe and welcoming pedestrian and bicycle entryways are necessary for North Side residents to access the environmental amenities and programs associated with the neighbouring Menomonee Valley, not to mention the employment opportunities presented by the renaissance of industry. Northside access issues are a focus of the *Valley 2.0 Plan.*

Localizing employment opportunities within environmental justice strategies remains a thorny challenge, as the Menomonee Valley case illustrates. In response, MVP is focusing on developing a place-based workforce strategy. Zetts (2015) describes other tactics such as career days where local kids visit factories, mentorship programs between local residents and employees with similar background stories, organizing presentations by employees in local schools to encourage potential candidates to submit applications and working on recruitment from the downtown Milwaukee Technical College for on-site training and placement opportunities. Although the energy for renewal of the Menomonee Valley came, in large part, from the surrounding communities that pushed for manufacturing as the land use and living wage as the workplace standard, the employment benefits are dispersed across the city and through Milwaukee's suburbs. While this challenge is not unique to environmental justice or Milwaukee, it does affirm that local benefits cannot be taken for granted, however worthy the intentions, and investments designed to benefit local residents may be captured further afield. The local economic revitalization potential is thus at serious risk of compromise without careful and very deliberate attention to the specific needs and circumstances characterizing local neighbourhoods. Further, there must be a sustained commitment to revisit and update strategies so that they remain nimble and responsive to existing and emerging barriers. Crafting goals and objectives for local employment, prioritizing construction contracts for EBE with local zip codes and simply building physical accessways are not enough to channel the thousands of high-quality manufacturing jobs to local residents.

Environmental justice work in the Menomonee Valley helped blunt the impact of deindustrialization, economic decline and typical Rust Belt socio-economic challenges. It did not solve these problems in total, but the scope of job creation is impressive, especially since these jobs are situated within the context of improvements to health, ecological habitat enhancement and creation of accessible greenspace in a marginalized downtown locale. What distinguishes the Menomonee Valley from other attempts to transform post-industrial urban environments into greenspace is re-industrialization and creation of quality jobs. It is also noteworthy that the transformation of a degraded and jettisoned downtown space could be deployed in service of Indigenous sovereignty and wellbeing in a community hundreds of kilometres away. Although daunting challenges to realizing the vision remain, the achievements are laudable. By virtue of coalition building among disparate stakeholders, the verve of the Forest County Potawatomi Community and leadership of the Sixteenth Street Community Centre, as well as the political willingness of elected officials, businesses and bureaucrats, the Menomonee Valley is an exemplar of how transformations in urban post-industrial greenspace can work across diverse interests and fields.

Bibliography

Akee, R. K. Q., Spilde, K. A., & Taylor, J. B. (2015). The Indian gaming regulatory act and its effects on American Indian economic development. *The Journal of Economic Perspectives; Nashville, 29*(3), 185–208.

Aten, N. (2008, July 23). Personal communication. In person.

Becker, A. (2015, December 16). Wisconsin's Black-White achievement gap worst in nation despite decades of efforts. *WisconsinWatch.org*. www.wisconsinwatch.org/2015/12/wisconsins-black-white-achievement-gap-worst-in-nation/.

Bray, L., Carlson, V., & Klovers, M. (2004). *Design and economic impact guidelines for the Menomonee Valley stockyards' redevelopment*. Menomonee Valley Partners.

Chadburn, M. (2017, March 6). Casinos create urban jobs, but at a price. *CityLab*. www.citylab.com/work/2017/03/why-casino-driven-development-is-a-roll-of-the-dice/518046/.

Chesters, G., Konrad, J. G., & Simsiman, G. V. (1979). *Menomonee river pilot watershed study summary and recommendations*. Environmental Protection Agency.

City of Milwaukee. (1998, October). *Market study, engineering, and land use plan for the Menomonee Valley*. Department of City Development, City of Milwaukee.

City of Milwaukee. (2004, December 6). City completes largest environmental clean up in history; Menomonee Valley site ready for business, recreation. *City of Milwaukee*. https://web.archive.org/web/20041206064708/http://mkedcd.org/news/2004/MRVcleanup.html.

City of Milwaukee, and Sixteenth Street Community Health Center. (2004). *Sustainability guidelines for the Menomonee River valley*. Menomonee Valley Partners.

Cook, C. (2015, July 9). Personal communication. In person.

Crawford, J. (2019, July 1). Personal communication. In person.

Daleiden, S. (2020). The Beerline trail: Milwaukee, Wisconsin. In W. Hood & G. M. Tada (Eds.), *Black landscapes matter*. University of Virginia Press.

Dennis, L. (2018, December 17). Hmong in Milwaukee seek the American dream. *WUWM 89.7*. www.wuwm.com/post/hmong-milwaukee-seek-american-dream.

Denvir, D. (2011, March 29). The 10 most segregated urban areas in America. *Salon*. www.salon.com/2011/03/29/most_segregated_cities/.

Derks, M. (2014). *Potawatomi history | tribal histories*. Wisconsin Public Television. www.pbs.org/video/wpt-documentaries-potawatomi-history/.

Desmond, M. (2016). *Evicted: Poverty and profit in the American City*. Penguin.

De Sousa, C. (2011a). Greening the industrial district: Transforming Milwaukee's Menomonee Valley from a blighted Brownfield into a sustainable place to work and play. In M. I. Slavin (Ed.), *Sustainability in America's cities* (pp. 45–68). Island Press.

De Sousa, C. (2011b). *Milwaukee's Menomonee Valley: A sustainable re-industrialization best practice*. University of Illinois at Chicago, Institute for Environmental Science and Policy.

De Sousa, C. (2021). *Sustainable Brownfield development: Building a sustainable future on sites of our polluting past*. Routledge.

De Sousa, C., & Gramling, B. (2003). The Menomonee Valley benchmarking initiative: Identifying priorities, assessing conditions, and devising a sustainable vision for Milwaukee's Menomonee Valley. *The Wisconsin Geographer, 19*, 4–13.

Environmental Protection Agency. (1979). *The IJC Menomonee river watershed study*. United States Environmental Protection Agency.

Environmental Protection Agency. (2006). *Case study in tribal water quality standards programs: The Sokaogon Chippewa community*. United States Environmental Protection Agency.

Foltman, L., & Jones, M. (2019, February 28). How redlining continues to shape racial segregation in Milwaukee. *WisContext*. www.wiscontext.org/how-redlining-continues-shape-racial-segregation-milwaukee.

Fredricksen, L. (2004, January 21). Annual survey of mining companies: 2003–2004. *Fraser Institute*. http://bit.ly/1LFwLdo.

Frey, W. H. (2018, December 17). Black-White segregation edges downward since 2000, census shows. *Brookings* (blog). www.brookings.edu/blog/the-avenue/2018/12/17/black-white-segregation-edges-downward-since-2000-census-shows/.

Geenen, P. H. (2014). *Civil rights activism in Milwaukee: South side struggles in the 60s and 70s*. The History Press.

Greer, D. M., Baumgardener, D. J., Bridgewatter, F. D., Frazer, D. A., Kessler, C. L., LeCounte, E. S., Swain, G. R., & Cisler, R. A. (2013). *Milwaukee health report 2013: Health disparities in Milwaukee by socioeconomic status*. Center for Urban Population Health.

Grossman, Z. (2017). *Unlikely alliances: Native nations and white communities join to defend rural lands*. University of Washington Press.

Gurda, J. (2008). *The making of Milwaukee* (3rd ed.). Milwaukee County Historical Society.

Gurda, J. (2021, June 30). After more than a century, Burnham canal, one of Milwaukee's deadest of dead zones, is being revived as a wetland. *Milwaukee Journal Sentinel*. www.jsonline.com/story/opinion/2021/06/30/burnham-canal-milwaukee-dead-zone-being-revived-wetland/7783170002/.

Holmes, I. (2019, July 10). Racism: Milwaukee's public health emergency. *Progressive.org*. https://progressive.org/api/content/c413d518-a1b7-11e9-8633-12f1225286c6/.

Hornik, K., Cutts, B., & Greenlee, A. (2016). Community theories of change: Linking environmental justice to stakeholder perceptions in Milwaukee (WI, USA). *International Journal of Environmental Research and Public Health, 13*(10), 1–17.

Johnson, E. (2020, June 21). COVID-19 shutdown of Potawatomi gaming exacted 'devastating' widespread toll. *The Journal Times*. https://journaltimes.com/news/local/covid-19-shutdown-of-potawatomi-gaming-exacted-devastating-widespread-toll/article_7e5fd338-3579-5250-9793-b90c707d81f7.html.

Kress, T. (2008, July 22). Personal communication. In person.

Leichenger, A. (2014, March 20). How one Milwaukee zip code explains America's mass incarceration problem. *Think Progress*. https://thinkprogress.org/how-one-milwaukee-zip-code-explains-americas-mass-incarceration-problem-66a6535d1c4/.

Leinbach, K. (2015, July 13). Personal communication. In person.

Leinbach, K. (2018). *Urban ecology: A natural way to transform kids, parks, cities, and the world.* Morgan James Publishing.

Levine, M. V. (2008). *The crisis continues: Black male joblessness in Milwaukee*. University of Wisconsin – Milwaukee, Center for Economic Development.

Levine, M. V. (2016, April). *Latino Milwaukee: A statistical portrait*. University of Wisconsin – Milwaukee, Center for Economic Development.

Levine, M. V. (2019). *Milwaukee 53206: The anatomy of concentrated disadvantage in an inner city neighborhood, 2000–2017*. Center for Economic Development Publications, 48, 70.

Levy, J. (2019, May 13). Potawatomi hotel & casino gives back to the local community as it grows. *Milwaukee Journal Sentinel*. www.jsonline.com/story/sponsor-story/potawatomi-hotel-and-casino/2019/05/13/potawatomi-hotel-casino-gives-back-local-community-grows/1143528001/.

Losen, D., Hodson, C., Keith, M. A., Morrison, K., & Belway, S. (2015, February 23). Are we closing the school discipline gap? *The Civil Rights Project at UCLA*. https://civilrightsproject.ucla.edu/resources/projects/center-for-civil-rights-remedies/school-to-prison-folder/federal-reports/are-we-closing-the-school-discipline-gap.

Lovely, L. (2001, July 2). *Milwaukee's old sixth street viaduct yields to modern cable-stayed spans.* www.constructionequipmentguide.com/milwaukees-old-sixth-street-viaduct-yields-to-modern-cable-stayed-spans/1384.

Loyd, J., & Bonds, A. (2018). Where do Black lives matter? Race, stigma, and place in Milwaukee, Wisconsin. *The Sociological Review, 66*(4), 898–918.

Massey, D. S., & Denton, N. A. (1998). *American apartheid: Segregation and the making of the underclass*. Harvard University Press.

Maternowski, M., & Powers, J. (2017, March 3). How did metro Milwaukee become so segregated? *WUWM 89.7*. www.wuwm.com/regional/2017-03-03/how-did-metro-milwaukee-become-so-segregated.

McAvoy, P. V., Driscoll, M. B., & Gramling, B. (2004). Integrating the environment, the economy, and community health: A Community Health Center's initiative to link health benefits to smart growth. *American Journal of Public Health, 94*(2), 525–527.

McKee, I. (1939). The centennial of 'the trail of death.' *Indiana Magazine of History, 35*(1), 27–41.

Menomonee Valley Partners. (2004). *Development objectives for the Menomonee Valley stockyards.* Menomonee Valley Partners.

Mock, B. (2015, October 30). Why Milwaukee is the worst place to live for African Americans. *Bloomberg CityLab.* www.bloomberg.com/news/articles/2015-10-30/milwaukee-is-the-worst-place-for-african-americans-because-of-county-sheriff-david-clarke.

Nenn, C. (2008, July 22). Personal communication. In person.

North Central Wisconsin Regional Planning Commission. (2011). *Forest County Potawatomi comprehensive plan.* Author. www.ncwrpc.org/forest/potawatomi/Potawatomi%20Comp Plan%20Adopted%202011_OnWeb.pdf.

Pabst, G. (2013, January 6). Report shows growth in Hmong Community. *Milwaukee Journal Sentinel.* www.jsonline.com/news/milwaukee/report-shows-growth-in-hmong-community-a388pb6-185823661.html.

Pember, M. A. (2019, March 8). Death by civilization. *The Atlantic.* www.theatlantic.com/education/archive/2019/03/traumatic-legacy-indian-boarding-schools/584293/.

Peterangelo, J., & Henken, R. (2014). *Redevelopment in Milwaukee's Menomonee valley: What worked and why?* Public Policy Forum.

Pettygrove, M., & Ghose, R. (2018). From 'rust belt' to 'fresh coast': Remaking the city through food justice and urban agriculture. *Annals of the American Association of Geographers, 108*(2), 591–603.

Prison Policy Initiative. (2019). Prison policy initiative: Wisconsin profile. *Prison Policy Initiative.* www.prisonpolicy.org/profiles/WI.html.

Reeves, R. V., & Rodrigue, E. (2016, February 17). Milwaukee, segregation, and the echo of welfare reform. *Brookings: Social Mobility Memos* (blog). www.brookings.edu/blog/social-mobility-memos/2016/02/17/milwaukee-segregation-and-the-echo-of-welfare-reform/.

Richards, E. (2015, March 1). State's Black suspension rate highest for high schools. *Milwaukee Journal Sentinel.* www.jsonline.com/news/education/wisconsin-black-suspension-rate-highest-in-us-for-high-schools-b99451618z1-294596321.html.

Richards, E., & Mulvany, L. (2014, May 17). 60 years after Brown v. Board of Education, intense segregation returns. *Milwaukee Journal Sentinel,* sec. Education. https://archive.jsonline.com/news/education/60-years-after-brown-v-board-of-education-intense-segregation-returns-b99271365z1-259682171.html/.

Seppa, N. (1994, February 11). Old foes now allies: Indians, sport fishermen join to oppose mine. *Wisconsin State Journal* (p. 1A).

Shambarger, E. (2015, July 11). Personal communication. In person.

Silver, M. *Poverty, race & Milwaukee: Unpacking new U.S. Census estimates.* Retrieved September 6, 2019, from www.wuwm.com/post/poverty-race-milwaukee-unpacking-new-us-census-estimates.

Smalkoski, K., Herther, N. K., Xiong, Z. B., Ritsema, K., Vang, R., & Zheng, R. (2012). Health disparities research in the Hmong American community: Implications for practice and policy. *Hmong Studies Journal, 13*(2), 31.

Smeeding, T. M., & Thornton, K. (2018). *Poverty, incomes, race and ethnicity in Wisconsin and Milwaukee: A supplement to the 2016 Wisconsin poverty report.* Institute for Research on Poverty.

Spivak, C. (2017, September 4). Gambling revenue flat as Potawatomi tribe wins about $400 million from gamblers. *Milwaukee Journal Sentinel.* www.jsonline.com/story/news/local/milwaukee/2017/09/04/revenue-flat-potawatomi-tribe-wins-400-million-gamblers/629116001/.

Sussman, M. (2018, November 20). The greening of Menomonee Valley. *Shepherd Express.* https://shepherdexpress.com/api/content/a8438316-ed07-11e8-939b-120e7ad5cf50/.

Tchakirides, W. (2018, June 3). Long before Sterling Brown's arrest, Milwaukee struggled with a policing problem. *Washington Post*. www.washingtonpost.com/news/made-by-history/wp/2018/06/03/long-before-sterling-browns-arrest-milwaukee-struggled-with-a-policing-problem/.

Timm, B. (2008, July 22). Personal communication. In person.

Tuck, E., & Wayne Yang, K. (2012). Decolonization is not a metaphor. *Decolonization: Indigeneity, Education & Society*, *1*(1), 1–40.

U. S. Census Bureau. *American FactFinder – results*. Retrieved September 9, 2019, from https://factfinder.census.gov/faces/tableservices/jsf/pages/productview.xhtml?src=bkmk.

U.S. Census Bureau. (n.d.). *Annual estimates of the resident population by sex, race, and hispanic origin for the United States, States, and counties: April 1, 2010 to July 1, 2018*. U.S. Census Bureau, Population Division.

Vang, C. Y. (2016). *Transforming a community for action: Hmong Americans in the Milwaukee area*. The Hmong Milwaukee Civic Engagement Project.

Welte, J. W., Wieczorek, W. F., Barnes, G. M., Tidwell, M.-C., & Hoffman, J. H. (2004). The relationship of ecological and geographic factors to gambling behavior and pathology. *Journal of Gambling Studies*, *20*(4), 405–423.

White, S., Zipp, J., Reynolds, P., and Paetsch, J. (1988). *The changing Milwaukee industrial structure, 1979–1988*. University of Wisconsin – Milwaukee Urban Research Center.

Whitehead, B. D. (2014, June 21). Gaming the poor. *Opinionator* (blog). https://opinionator.blogs.nytimes.com/2014/06/21/gaming-the-poor/.

Wisconsin Department of Transportation. (1995). Milwaukee east-west corridor transportation study, major investment study/draft environmental impact statement, Milwaukee, Wisconsin: Deliverable . . . Wisconsin Department of Transportation, District No. 2.

Woodard, C. (2016). How Milwaukee shook off the rust. *Politico Magazine*. www.politico.com/magazine/story/2016/08/milwaukee-what-works-industrial-clean-up-214174.

Zetts, C. (2008, July 23). Personal communication. In person.

Zetts, C. (2015, July 13). Personal communication. In person.

4

LA PETITE CEINTURE

Paris, France

What happens when long, linear circuits that are exhausted of their industrial uses are then completely neglected by the landowner? How about when the landowner is part of the massive state infrastructure, and the site extends for 32 km through the "capital of modernity," Paris? In the previous chapter, an expansive downtown portion of Milwaukee became derelict and isolated, until a coalition of Indigenous, civic and community-based actors shaped a massive green re-industrialization strategy. But in Paris' Petite Ceinture, a rail line dedicated to the city's extensive industrial network for over 130 years, greenspace creation evolved in a different direction, a less coordinated direction that produced critical ecological habitat and otherwise unavailable socio-cultural opportunities. Although the entire rail line remains under the ownership and ultimate control of France's national rail line, the Petit Ceinture offers unique ecosystems that are meaningful for people who are peripheral to the mainstream. While its visibility has risen in the past decade, becoming a magnet for savvy Parisian naturalists and flaneurs, the Petite Ceinture's standing as a greenspace serving subaltern and marginalized communities distinguishes it as a self-assembling, indeterminate corridor that severs the regulation of urban space.

As the volume of freight traffic along the Petite Ceinture dwindled through the late twentieth century, the intensity of daily disturbance also attenuated. With fewer and fewer heavy trains rolling by, plants and animals were able to spend longer stretches of time between disturbance events, and the overall volume of train line personnel working along the tracks also plummeted. The rail company was unconcerned with anything beyond the most basic track maintenance, and the verges that previously had been kept free of vegetation transitioned to meadows and then shrubs and trees. New inhabitants settled in, both non-human and human, as ecological succession advanced with successive waves of urban de-industrialization. Meanwhile, the demand for cargo rail infrastructure in general dried up across the country, and consecutive segments of the loop were decommissioned and left untended. The tracks were periodically cleared of woody vegetation, and nobody appeared bothered by the messy, overgrown weedscape.

DOI: 10.4324/9781315106403-4

FIGURE 4.1   Petite Ceinture vista, 2011

Source: Image by J. Foster

Combined with an overall shift from rail to truck carriage, by the early 1990s, rail transport was completely shut down along the Petite Ceinture. This included the deactivation of the intensive maintenance regime that groomed the corridor. For over a century, heavy rail operational prerogatives like quick drainage, flat surfaces and clear sightlines dominated the ecology. Now it was finally left for wild. Seeds germinated, and new cycles of ecological succession progressed unhindered, including the emergence of novel ecosystems distinct from any historic referents. By 2005, for those aware of the line's efflorescence, it became known as *le plus vaste jardin secret de Paris*, the most extensive unknown garden in Paris (Lamming, 2005, p. 101). Lots of people also found refuge, and the vast loop quickly evolved outside the mandate of municipal or any formal planning strategies. But like most unclaimed spaces in western metropolises, the Petite Ceinture did not remain inconspicuous for long.

Today, the Petite Ceinture is a major preoccupation of Paris nature-lovers, urban explorers, historians, activists, planners and elected officials. Not surprisingly, local residents across each of the prefectures it intersects have strong feelings about the rail line as well. Every year new portions, ranging from a few hundred metres to several kilometres, become publicly accessible and are managed according to municipal design standards. Some portions are heavily altered with uniform synthetic engineered surfacing, while others have been adapted as community outdoor amenities like allotment gardens. Yet, for more than two precious decades, it remained completely fallow, or to use the French term, it existed among the *délaissés urbains*. And the majority of the line remains as such, undefined in relation to intensively settled surroundings, in a prolonged transitional state that is ecologically self-enriching and open to creatively clandestine usage.

Many non-Parisians would still be surprised to find out that a 32-km-long belt of green hugs the city's inner edges. In fact, most Parisians themselves were largely unaware of this ecological attribute until rather recently, when it rose to prominence through the launch of extensive public consultation about the line's future in 2016. The Petite Ceinture may have been better known 50 years ago, in its previous incarnation as a means of transporting industrial materials around the city. It was designed for freight efficiency, never crossing a roadway but circling the whole city. It also connects Paris' five major radial rail spurs. It crosses the Seine twice, as well as the Canal de l'Ourcq. In short, it furnishes the perfect terrestrial circuit through any city: unobstructed and continuous, discrete yet efficient, contained and self-sufficient. And these are the very elements that made it an incredible ecological refuge once the rail company finally ceased operations and relinquished active land management in 1993. With time, these attributes also made it into a refuge for people seeking recreation and livelihood opportunities otherwise unavailable in the city.

The succession of the rail line from heavy industry to verdant oasis presents new strategies for environmental justice that emphasize informality, vacancy, aesthetic disorder and appreciation of places known as *terrain vague*. The ways that varied communities respond to an unplanned greenspace in these former industrial lands, particularly at the neighbourhood scale and in their immediate environs, reveal a great deal about equity, justice and the "right to the city" in Paris. The Petite Ceinture is an exceptional greenspace, where purportedly degraded land yields vast habitat richness and unique socio-cultural opportunities. The evolution of the rail line as an interstitial space peripheral to the mainstream suggests ways that alternate experiences of urbanity that are critical to creating an equitable, inclusive and sustainable city may be ecologically determined through unplanned greenspace.

Setting the stage for ecological succession

The Petite Ceinture predates Paris' metro system by almost half a century. From 1854 to 1993, it provided a means for steam trains to transport materials from abattoirs, automobile factories, munitions and defence plants, wine depots, quarries and other industrial assemblages within the city, into the French provinces and further afield. It also conveyed basic supplies into the city that were essential to people's sustenance, like livestock for the slaughterhouses in Paris' northeast. In the early days, it provided passenger transportation, concentrated along the city's western edges with trains running every 30 minutes (Menant, 2017). The loop was opened in stages, and the final piece was completed in 1869. In its fully operational heyday, it served 23 stations, and the complete tour of the city took 1 hour and 21 minutes (Bretelle, 2015). When the freight-free, modern, electric metro system opened in 1900, passenger operations along the Petite Ceinture fell into steep decline. Unsurprisingly, Parisians overall preferred the clean, tiled subway stations linked to the metropolitan centre over the Petite Ceinture's industrial stations servicing only the edges of the city. By 1934, there were no more passenger cars on the line. Except for the sporadic "discovery tours" of historians and train buffs (Terrier & Delziani, 2018), the Petite Ceinture became dedicated to freight traffic servicing the industrial perimeter of Paris and the trunk lines connecting the city with the world beyond.

Beginning in the 1980s, the impacts of economic globalization sent Paris' industrial economy into decline. The car factories closed, the abattoirs moved out of town, manufacturers shut down and small ateliers dwindled. Meanwhile, there was a shift in the popularity of trucks as a means of goods transport. With ununionized drivers and flexible routes, more and more of the carriage business went to trucks. Rail freight traffic trickled to a crawl. As chronicled by Terrier and Delziani (2018), beginning in the 1970s, stations were progressively closed until circulation was distilled to only a few stations, with gradual melting of the trunk lines from freight into high-speed passenger bullet train capacity. Eventually, the national train company, *Société nationale des chemins de fer français* (SNCF) sought to sell the Petite Ceinture. However, the state prohibited any sale and insisted that it remains a public asset that can accommodate usage should the rail service be revived (Foster, 2010). Consequently, ownership was locked with an agency that no longer had any use for the land. The only management provision was preservation of conditions for the remote possibility that regular train service might revive along the tracks.

In practice, all that this meant was that the main pathway had to remain clear and rails could not be removed. Beyond those stipulations, the SNCF did not seem to be particularly concerned about the condition of the Petite Ceinture and simply withdrew all additional maintenance. The tracks could buckle and warp and become misaligned and unstable. As long as they were not intentionally removed, the state was satisfied.

When the SNCF desisted management of the Petite Ceinture, ecological succession quickly took hold and progressed in unique and fascinating ways. Although the SNCF did occasionally sweep through with herbicides as a means of controlling tree growth between the rails, for the most part, this was limited to the tracks alone and not the surrounding banks, verges and wider corridors. Once stations and gates were sealed, the Petite Ceinture was essentially left as is. As a result, nature could prosper undisturbed. Plants could root, pools of water could form, biomass could accumulate and animals could roam. Conditions could not have been more ideal for an emerging ecological asset in a dense city.

In addition to being vacated of freight train interference, another set of ecological advantages enabled the Petite Ceinture to flourish. It is connected to two large forests on opposite sides of Paris. To the west is the 850-hectare Bois de Boulogne, the ancient royal forest and hunting ground that features lakes, ponds, streams and a water reservoir, as well as a constructed waterfall and recreational

FIGURE 4.2 Petite Ceinture trench and tunnel, 2017

Source: Image by J. Foster

and sports facilities (including the famous Longchamps horseracing track and the Stade Roland Garros tennis complex). To the east, the Petite Ceinture adjoins the 1,000-hectare Bois de Vincennes, another ancient forest and royal hunting preserve with lakes, gardens and recreational and sports facilities (as well as horse and bicycle racing tracks). The Petite Ceinture became a highly traversed conduit between these two expansive greenspaces, facilitating species mobility across the two ends of the city. This wasn't just a series of stepping-stone style patches of green that environmental planners typically dream of squeezing into the urban fabric to enrich urban habitat connectivity. This was a dedicated highway network.

As soon as the rail line ceased operation the two immense forests began functioning as population sources, with flora and fauna moving into and along the tracks. In addition to these large closed-canopy forests with interior habitat, the Petite Ceinture also links other major parks and gardens. The route intersects, for example, with the parcs André Citroën, Georges Brassens, Montsouris, Buttes Chaumont, des Batignolles, de Villette and Martin Luther King, as well as the Coulée Vert (also known as the *Promenade Planté*), jardins du Ranelagh and square Charles Péguy. Predictably, it wasn't long before its ecological function evolved from conduit between the established greenspaces to habitat in and of itself where fauna could fulfil their entire lifecycle needs right on the rail line. Thus, within a few years, animals were no longer just using the Petite Ceinture as a convenient pathway, and habitat quality had improved to the extent that animals were settling onto the tracks as their predominant range and breeding grounds. Dense vegetative coverage was established by an invasion of flora common across Paris, such as *douce-amère* (Bittersweet or *Solanum dulcamara*), *armoise* (Mugwort or *Artemesia absinthium*, integral to the famous French alcoholic spirit Absinthe), *renouée du Japon* (Japanese knotweed or *Polygonum cuspidatum*), ruine de Rome (Ivy-leaved toadflax or *Cymbalaria muralis*) as well as various birch, maple and locust trees.

In a short time, early successional stage herbs and grasses gave way to patches of closed-canopy forest with *roncier* (briar) understories. The Petite Ceinture began to develop some structural diversity, with multiple layers of vegetation creating a more complex ecosystem that could sustain more varied fauna. As a former rail line, drainage was a primary consideration in the early construction requisites. This is evident in the gravel substrate that remains today, designed to wick the soil strata to a parched state so surface water depletes quickly and trains could move unimpeded. Combined with the typical conditions of fallow land in the regional Île-de-France landscape setting, the flora that has established along the tracks evolved into novel ecologies without historic precedence. Fusing the legacy of intensive rail management with an almost fully "hands off" approach furnished the conditions for a new type of urban wilderness to emerge. There was no guiding vision of what it should look like, how it should function or who should inhabit the corridor. Without design intervention or ongoing management, the ecological conditions on the Petite Ceinture were free to self-assemble. It became a quintessential novel ecology. The historic conditions of industrialization remained unmistakable, evident in the tracks, signals, stations, buffers and linear landscape form itself. But the ecological systems that evolved year by year were completely distinct from any antecedent. This is an outstanding instance of nature reconstituting itself where the primary conditions of life – the mineral composition, the hydrology, the microclimates, and the concentration of worrisome contaminants – have been deeply altered by human activity over multiple generations and where ecological integrity is commensurate with species invasion.

Overlayed with the built infrastructure and chemical saturation of over 100 years of industrial activity, the habitat combinations and opportunities are truly unique. A study by the Paris planning bureau, Atelier Parisien d'Urbanisme (APUR), found that by 2011, the tracks hosted over 1,000 plant species, 1,000 species of lichens and mushrooms, a dozen slug and terrestrial mollusc species and over 1,000 insect species. The study also found that Petite Ceinture was the only viable habitat in Paris for a large colony of rare and protected bats (*Pipistrellus pipistrellus*) living in its tunnels, as well as a protected species of wall lizard (*Podarcis muralis*). The study concludes that by 2011, the Petite Ceinture's ecological significance equalled the city's two major woodlands (APUR, 2011). A further 2017 study by the city's Urban Ecology Agency and SNCF focusing on ecological services of the 47.8 hectares of permeable surface occupied by the rail line confirmed the high level of biodiversity permeating the tracks (Mairie de Paris et SNCF, 2017). After completing detailed species inventories of ten train stations as well as a selection of covered areas, the study provides an analysis of the rail line's ecological continuity and recommendations for supporting biodiversity. Based on 590 species observations (including 21 species of nesting birds and 5 species of bats), the study creates a cartography of priority habitats. These include, for instance, prairies, uncultivated fields, large expanses of indigenous shrubs, brambles, standing snags and stone walls. The study also identifies a high level of habitat continuity, based on the combination of ecosystem types represented on the rail line and primary ("functional"), secondary and tertiary ("relay") patches that compose the landscape matrix within which the rapidly evolving ecosystem types are immersed. The analytical inventory finds that the Petite Ceinture is an original and unique ecological asset that is highly adaptable and resilient, with habitat areas that could be enriched as well as that should be preserved without modification. In particular, the dark portions of the rail line, where tunnels create lightless conditions, are exceptional habitats worthy of protection as is. Among many recommendations, the study advises protecting the rail line's diverse ecosystems as a continuous channel, augmenting habitat overall, vegetizing the over 50 km of vertical fencing, walls and grating and advancing ecological inventories through public participation (Mairie de Paris et SNCF, 2017).

After trains stopped rolling, debates about the post-freight disposition of the Petite Ceinture were subdued. For the first few years, when it was newly decommissioned, discussion was nominal and wasn't captured in the broad public realm. The rail company simply ceased operations and shuttered the remaining stations. Fencing was erected, and structures like tool storage sheds, buffer stops and signal lamps were left in place. There was little fanfare. Rather, the tracks and surrounding verges just settled, devoid of administrative attention or ongoing physical maintenance. The tracks were also more or less out of the gaze of the bustling pedestrians crossing over and under it as they went about their daily business. Parts emerge in spectacular locales, such as through the deep and wide trenches of the Parc Buttes Chaumont, where a vast gypsum quarry supplied the city's plaster until the mid-1860s (and before that, the area served as dumping grounds for animal carcasses and livestock waste). But in 1993, after the last train rolled along the track, few people took notice of the Petite Ceinture, much less articulated a vision for its future. It was merely derelict land that the SNCF had not yet dealt with, an eyesore that enclosed the city's inner edges. It was largely disregarded. It was easy to bypass, and its positioning around the edges of the city kept it out of popular pathways for tourism. On the fringes of the city, amid disused industrial lands, the Petite Ceinture was not at all a civic preoccupation. As Strohmayer and Corre (2012) explain,

> there was and continues to be considerably less pressure onto the space occupied by the Ceinture than on other, comparable spaces within an urban context: areas zoned for commercial or residential real estate and incorporated into for-profit organisational structures do not, on average, stay vacant for as long as the Ceinture did.
>
> *(4)*

Today, visitors to the rail line might encounter mid-sized mammals such as domestic and stray cats, hedgehogs (*Erinaceus europaeus*), foxes (*Vulpes vulpes*) and beech martens (*Mates foina*). Birds such as winter wren (*Troglodytes hiemalis*), Eurasian blackcap (*Sylvia atricapilla*) and common chiffchaff (*Phylloscopus collybita*) are also easily spotted. The Petite Ceinture even features in renowned birdwatcher and nature broadcaster David Lindo's (2015) popular book *Tales From the Concrete Jungles*, where he notes species such as Spotted Flycatcher (*Muscicapa striata*), Ring Ouzel (*Turdus torquatus*), Sparrowhawk (*Accipiter nisus*), Peregrine falcon (*Falco peregrinus*) and Crested Tit (*Lophophanes cristatus*). Especially along the more walled-in portions of the rail line, where tracks are furrowed into sunken trenches, walking along the corridor feels like full submersion in nature. The sounds of the city can feel distant, even if they originate only a few metres away, space can feel less compressed and songbirds intermingle with the hushed sway of leaves and grasses. Along the raised segments, particularly the bridges crossing the Seine and the Canal de l'Ourcq, the expansive perspective from the tracks can be stunning. The vista opens on both sides, and the city's surface hydrology is put on brilliant display, illuminating how water flows into, through and beyond Paris. These are unique experiences of the city, and they are emblematic of the appeal of the Petite Ceinture for legions of urban ecologists and explorers.

Terra nullius and the planning imagination

Environmental planning in Paris spotlights the Petit Ceinture while bypassing the issue of land ownership by the national rail company. Commenting on the line's perceived vacancy as equivalent to a "blank slate" on land in an ancient, heavily populated city, O'Sullivan (2016) notes that "Ringing inner Paris without actually passing through its heart, re-opening the line for public access is the sort of rare chance that doesn't come a city's way twice." Reviewing the documents guiding visions and plans for the line, it is as though the expansive space was completely absorbed into the public domain and available for a new transformation. In the few instances where the rail company is mentioned, information about the SNCF entitlement to return freight or some other form of rail usage is generally missing. Without decreeing firm policies for the disposition of the land, there is a tendency in contemporary planning related to the Petite Ceinture to celebrate its specific attributes as they pertain to the surrounding landscape and elevate these as sustainability accomplishments. In particular, the Petite Ceinture's abilities to furnish landscape continuity and biodiversity opportunities for the city garner pronounced attention. Yet, in terms of civic imagination, the Petite Ceinture also plays into other competing visions, depending on the agency seeking to fulfil its mandate. In some instances, it is an environmental asset. At other points, from the perspective of other agencies, it is enmeshed in strategies for housing development, as conveniently located construction staging areas, or as the ideal space for services like medical facilities, daycares or recreation centres.

The rail line first appears as an urban environmental asset with the city's 2011 biodiversity plan. In general, urban biodiversity plans tend to focus on the breadth of species represented in discrete spatial features. But in the case of the Petite Ceinture, the strategic value of the combined spatial extent and configuration brought it to the forefront of the city's vision for the future. The 2011 plan attends to three priorities: reinforcing ecological continuity, integrating biodiversity into sustainable development, and enhancing public ecological literacy. The Petite Ceinture is ideally suited to respond to each of these, not just within the city's administrative boundaries but also according to trajectories of species movement across the region. In terms of reinforcing ecological continuity, the rail line is paired with the banks of the Boulevard Périphérique (an autoroute circling the outer edges of the city) as an ecological beacon, and the stated goal is to "create a veritable green belt around Paris, with the Petite Ceinture and the *périphérique* embankments linking a vast ring of green spaces, creating an interface that relays Parisian and neighboring natural terrain and connects these zones to regional biodiversity sources" (Marie de Paris, 2011, p. 4). Speaking on the need to mobilize that biodiversity plan at the neighbourhood scale, Marc Prochasson (2011), the Coordinator of Sustainability, Climate and Environment Coordinator for the city's 20th arrondissement, relates

> Every time something happens on the Petite Ceinture there are reactions from inhabitants, like if there is a train or if there are temporarily parked buses they will complain about the noise. There are people who will complain about the shadow of the trees. If we cut a tree there will be other people saying that we are destroying nature. We recently approved a biodiversity plan for Paris, and we included a debate about the future of the Petite Ceinture.

We need to explain to people why the space is interesting, so each year we organize visits for neighbors. That way if the RATP claims that they park buses because the space is not interesting, neighbors can respond "well I visited and I know that it is replete with biodiversity." If we want to organize the debate, we have to inform inhabitants about the richness of the environment.

The critical role of the Petite Ceinture as a vector of ecological continuity and species dispersal was affirmed in 2013, with the regional *Schéma Régional de Cohérence Ecologique* that articulated plans for a blue-green corridor strategy that combines aquatic and terrestrial networks (Préfet de la Région d'Île-de-France, 2013). Likewise, the Petite Ceinture figured prominently in the 2017 regional green plan, which aimed to establish 500 new hectares of new green space by 2021. By 2019, the City updated its biodiversity plan according to three axes: infusing biodiversity into all urban planning strategies and construction projects to create an engaged populace ensuring that biodiversity is accessible to and supported by all; and thinking about the city as a biodiversity asset. The Petite Ceinture dovetails right into this updated plan, evident in recommendations ranging from targeted financial investment, classification of certain sites as *Espace Naturels Sensibles* (sensitive natural areas), conserving the rail line from future developments, reinforcing links between the Petite Ceinture and neighbouring greenspaces and creating a nocturnal biodiversity inventory and mapping nocturnal species mobility paths. Further, it corresponds with recommendations for enhancing the permeability of fences and walls, establishing an Ecotourism Department in order to help residents and tourists appreciate the city's living heritage, registering with the regional bat and dragonfly action plan and monitoring protected and threatened species. The Petite Ceinture also features prominently in the regional bat protection plan of 2012–16, particularly in terms of an inventory of the rail line and the work completed by the insertion agencies. All of these perspectives are relayed in the regional biodiversity plan for 2019–2030, which refocused the lens towards improving health and well-being through nature, making biodiversity an economic asset, putting biodiversity at the core of territorial management and protecting nature as *notre capital commun* (our shared capital).

Despite the sincerity of these plans, it remains unclear whether the dominant proprietor is on board. The SNCF, after all, continues to insist that the tracks remain clear. And as landscape architect Germain Lainard reveals in the video *De la Jungle au Jardins de Traverses sur la Petite Ceinture-Paris 18e* (2019), projects are provisional and the SNCF requires that they must be designed to be dismantled upon only 60 days notice. Although the SNCF remains committed to the partnerships with insertion agencies, these are valorized as collaborations in the interest of maintenance, experimentation and sustainable management of the tracks. Ecological attributes of the Petite Ceinture are referenced by the SNCF primarily in relation to landscape management agreements with insertion agencies. For instance, the 2016 SNCF review of the first ten years of partnership with insertion agencies presents economic and social welfare advances as fundamental, and biodiversity and sustainability are auspicious by-products. The ecological attributes of the Petite Ceinture are approached as reasons to adapt rail management techniques, rather than preserving the space as *terrain vague* or dedicated ecological habitat, explained thus:

> The Petite Ceinture is an atypical rail site, and a different form of management is appropriate in these urban green spaces: manual and mechanical, without herbicides, this management method is intended to be more gentle and respectful of the environment.
>
> *(SNCF, 2016, p. 16)*

The commitment to restore potential train service is not always evident in the actual maintenance that the SNCF conducts on the Petite Ceinture. At Porte d'Ivry, the bridge was reconstructed without integrating any tracks whatsoever, to a standard that cannot support trains. In some parts of the Petite Ceinture, the SNCF has completely set aside concern over ecological management techniques, in favour of infrastructure support for ongoing construction projects. For instance, in 2017 in 13th arrondissement, the rails were removed along an exposed trench and the surface was covered in asphalt. An open-air bentonite processing plant was installed where the tracks once ran, turning it into a construction staging area with massive silos, conveyors, feed bins, grinding and mixing machines and pipelines that transport materials through the tunnel to nearby construction sites. The bentonite processing site is overseen by the municipal transportation agency Régie Autonome des Transports Parisiens (RATP), which is working to modernize its real estate portfolio of 750 hectares of industrial lands, to include multi-purpose office buildings, maintenance facilities, housing units and public facilities like senior and day-care centres. In 2014, the municipal transportation agency (RATP) agreed to build 2000 new housing units on its industrial lands, half of which would be social housing. The approach is known as "real estate development without land acquisition," an approach that seeks to enhance the value of existing property holdings such that they become self-financing operations. An example along the Petite Ceinture is the Jourdan-Corentin-Issoire workshops in the 14th arrondissement, which includes 650 housing units (191 of which are social housing, 365 are for students and 108 are private) built above an extended bus depot with a 1.2-hectare greenroof garden (Feredj, 2016). In these spaces, the transit agency is able to accumulate capital through all forms of rent, offset the operation costs for its facilities and even gain surplus revenue. Working in conjunction with SNCF, the municipal transit authority has become a leading player in the provision of new housing in Paris.

The City signed an official agreement with SNCF in 2006, a protocol that spells out the terms of partnership in sharing the rail line. The stated objectives of this agreement include preserving the main rail tracks, identifying areas suitable for adaptive management (such as gardens, promenades and public open space), exploring alternative approaches to recuring management challenges and evaluating opportunities for complementary use of stations and workshops on a case-by-case basis (RFF and Mairie de Paris, 2006).

FIGURE 4.3   Bentonite processing on the Petite Ceinture, 2019

Source: Image by J. Foster

In 2013, the City launched a public process to gather the perspectives of Parisians, which included consultative sessions with residents as well as interest and advocacy groups. After two years of process planning, building public awareness and outreach to potential participants, the consultation was, remarkably, completed within seven weeks between late December and mid-February. These consultations revolved around two sets of guiding questions, both designed as provocation to more open-ended and visionary discussions. The first set asked whether the possibility of train usage needs to be preserved, whether other temporary or permanent usages can be welcomed and under what conditions. The second set of questions elicited proposals to honour the nature, biodiversity, leisure and recreation values, culture, beauty and urban development possibilities beyond heavy rail. The consultations included dialogue through an online portal, five public meetings, five community-specific workshop meetings, 15 guided tours to enhance knowledge of the Petite Ceinture, a public seminar (with researchers, institutional actors and advocacy organizations) to deepen understanding of key issues, and a public gathering with elected officials to synthesize the key findings and debate possibilities. It is difficult to assess unique participants since the process is designed to continue engaging residents in sequential conversations. But the numbers are impressive: 2,435 online contributions, around 350 attendees at the five public meetings, 650 at the five community workshops, 400 partaking in the on-site tours, 200 participants in the public seminar series and 350 at the public synthesis debate with elected officials (known as *la reunion de restitution*).

As recounted in the final report on the consultations, few people proposed the development of the Petite Ceinture and its banks, and the majority were against this direction. There was major convergence around the conception of the Petite Ceinture as a social and "respiration" space in the city, with emphasis on the potential to learn how to "live together" through the Petite Ceinture (Mairie de Paris and RFF, 2013). Within the wide range of perspectives articulated through the consultative sessions, there were discussions around questions like governance of the space and management approaches, as well as the role of citizens and insertion agencies in managing and implementing the visions. Although there was wide variation within these views, in general participants' congregated around a desire for flexibility (reversibility) in management approaches, preserving the continuous linear infrastructure, conserving the industrial heritage and mixed uses in the widest sections of the Petite Ceinture. Some participants regretted that the process included only residents within Paris and excluded neighbours on the outside of the Petite Ceinture. There was also a sharp division between those advocating for return of train traffic (mostly online participants, some arguing in favour of an environmentally sensitive system combined with public transportation in the dense yet underserved northeast portion of the city and gardeners with access to plots alongside the rail line) and those opposed to the reintroduction of trains (mostly neighbouring residents concerned about the degradation of their quality of life). Others proposed occasional tourist trains or a recreational Velo-rail system. Nonetheless, there was a strong agreement that any decisions should celebrate the line's industrial heritage by restoring and utilizing the buildings and stations.

In terms of nature, while most support the management of the line as "*un espace de respiration*," there was a deep disagreement about the level of security necessary for the enjoyment of the space and the intensity of access compatible with the conservation of biodiversity. Shared gardens, urban agricultural production (including livestock and use of the tunnels as chilled storage warehouses), and a horticultural school were also popular proposals, supported by insertion agencies like Association Espaces as compatible with biodiversity preservation. Almost all participants agree on the priority of biodiversity protection, and some insisted that this must occur without management, so that "*la nature pourrait librement s'exprimer*" (nature can express itself freely). Interestingly, there was an agreement between ecologists and groups in favour of freight rail traffic, such as Association Sauvegard Petite Ceinture, that reviving train service is most compatible with biodiversity and the free expression of nature, as opposed to gardening and urban agriculture. The need to preserve routes for continuous species movement between large reserves is emphasized by researchers and ecological professionals as fundamental to biodiversity conservation. Nonetheless, the importance of ecological services was prioritized throughout the consultations, specifically in terms of surface permeability, thermal regulation and habitat patches within a densely settled city. Again, there were differences of opinion regarding the desirability of an open-access recreational

FIGURE 4.4   Petite Ceinture community gardens on verges, 2012

Source: Image by J. Foster

trail, specifically in terms of the negative impacts on habitat and biodiversity caused by human disturbances and the infrastructure necessary to ensure safe and universal access.

On the matter of learning to live together, there was much enthusiasm for non-commercial engagements, such as meeting spaces, shared gardens, educational studios and workshop and cooperative landscape management enterprises. The ideal of creating convivial opportunities that appeal to diverse residents in proximity to neighbourhoods gained a lot of support. But, perhaps unsurprisingly, the preferences of neighbours and those further afield clashed. Cultural and artistic engagements were popular, especially temporary or ephemeral events that connect with the Petite Ceinture's industrial heritage, such as concerts, neighbourhood fêtes, expositions, art installations and theatre spectacles. Many favoured "underground" and free expressions, such as opportunities for street art, that are not institutionally planned and overseen. Yet, residents living directly along the rail line expressed concern about security and noise. In response to concerns that management is unnecessary and the "unique" and "mythical" character of the rail line should be conserved, the final report summarized the opposing perspective of those living in proximity: "neighbours contend that the site needs to be cleaned, secure and surveyed in order to avoid malevolence as well as garbage on the tracks" (Mairie de Paris and RFF, 2013, p. 17). In the northeast portion of the line, some proposed construction of social housing in viable locations, or offering lodging within existing rail infrastructure and train cars. Despite overall opposition to construction on the tracks, there were reports that people have already invested deposits for the acquisition of apartments along a "future green pathway."

The consultative process generated vivid public exchange and certainly appears to have succeeded in raising awareness about the Petite Ceinture, urban ecological systems and civic engagement opportunities. The range of concrete ideas proposed is extraordinary, including inspired ideas like open-air cinemas in the tunnels, horse-drawn trains, downhill ski trails along the talus slopes, a cemetery, icehouses in the tunnels, sheep and goat pastures, a *via ferrata* network of suspended trails or fields of wheat, hops and poppy cultivation. The final report ends by confirming consensus around the desire not to turn this unusual, aesthetically compelling, biodiverse and historically rich site into a banal environment. A 2015 protocol followed, updating the joint objectives to encompass: 1) progressively opening portions of the Petite Ceinture in the south, southeast, east and northeast for public enjoyment; 2) enabling profitable development of portions of the tracks through leisure, cultural, economic, sport or gardening and agricultural activities; and 3) protecting and valorizing the natural, architectural and landscape heritage of the rail line. While this second protocol acknowledges the City's evaluation of the line as an ecological corridor and its integration in the Biodiversity Plan, it nonetheless asserts the priority of protecting continuity for trains (Mairie de Paris and RFF, 2015).

Rather than engaging in complex and intense development planning, the City simply started opening portions of the Petite Ceinture and welcoming people onto the tracks. Areas that had previously been fenced off were no longer prohibited, and visitors had City-approved alternatives to the network of clandestine access points. This was not particularly popular among some elected officials, who expected economic investment into their communities, not simple access to uncultivated space. However, as APUR Director Christiane Blancot (2017) explains, the City wanted to proceed with a light touch, by securing small sections and hiring animation teams on small budgets. The elected officials eventually acceded and dropped their appeals for investments in things like programs, apparatus and restaurants and agreed to support simply opening access before compiling plans. Blancot (2017) explains the City's perspective in managing the expectations of elected officials:

> They did something fairly classic. They composed programs and then told us "We want to fulfill this program and we want to develop to meet the needs of this program." But we told them "No. You must stop all of this." We had to explain to the elected officials that we made promises to people that we would follow this course. So fine, the answer is that we will open. And that's all. What people want deep down, it's not programs, they just want to visit. The most important thing is to visit, and to make the conditions for access. Right away.

Bruno Gouyette (2017), the City's lead administrator for the Petite Ceinture, describes the approach as "different from those who say that you have to open for walks and who do not always understand the project we make." In terms of governance, he comments that "We did not find the magic answer, but there is a dual piloting process," which is a steering committee that combines three deputies to the mayor, the deputy secretary general and four SNCF representatives. A second enlarged steering committee combines the elected representatives from the nine arrondissements crossed by the Petite Ceinture, all the groups of the Paris Council and invited political groups. Gouyette is also clear, however, that there is one important group that is not represented in the public consultations, official dialogue or governance model. These are the "transgressors." He categorizes transgressors into two groups: those who are tolerated, like graffiti artists and walkers smoking a joint, and those for whom there is less tolerance, such as tam-tam players and people who throw rocks.

There is another group, however, that falls in a shifting position along the continuum of public tolerance. Over the past decade, settlement of the Petite Ceinture by homeless residents has stirred intense debate and administrative response, especially when communities of unhoused residents claim visible segments of the tracks to form encampments.

Gradients of greenspace access

Today, an amalgam of restricted areas and formal trails determine official public access to the Petite Ceinture. Most of the line remains administratively off-limits to people. The tunnels are sealed behind iron barricades with industrial-strength bolt locks. Other portions of the line are confined within 2-m-high fencing, sometimes fortified with chain link and sometimes topped with razor wire. Yet entry points abound, however well concealed, for those seeking refuge. The stations and storage facilities prove particularly appealing to artists and functional for people in need of shelter. Some of the buildings are leased to artists for studio and commercial spaces, but many who inhabit the buildings are described as drifters, squatters or homesteaders, depending on the perspective concerning the property and the right to the city.

In the name of security, SNCF and municipal agents conduct periodic cycles of eviction and fence reinforcement, in the wake of which new entry points are soon creatively devised and old ones are unsealed. Gouyette (2017) identifies technical security as the second biggest challenge in managing the rail line, after jurisdictional strife. He explains that this remains a rail line with tracks, wires, tunnels and bridges that were not designed for public use and could, like any unrestricted industrial site, cause personal harm and legal issues for both the SNCF and City. Fires deep in the tunnels pose particular challenges, especially when fuel canisters spill or propane tanks explode. However, the practice of evicting people living on the Petite Ceinture is a more recent development that goes beyond technical security concerns. In 2011, Prochasson, a Mairie Coordinator in one of the city's disadvantaged north-east arrondissements, characterized residents as inconspicuous custodians, sometimes only perceptible thanks to carefully tended gardens along

FIGURE 4.5 Petite Ceinture homestead, 2012

Source: Image by J. Foster

the tracks, and also noted that there had always been people living on the Petite Ceinture, even through its industrial heyday.

By 2017, expansive encampments were in plain view along the Petite Ceinture. These became a major civic concern, especially in the city's northern and eastern arrondissements, especially with regard to Albanian and Bulgarian migrant communities. In a 2017 documentary video entitled *Le Petite Ceinture Refuge*, the coordinator of the municipal task force for people without a fixed address speaks about the challenges in removing communities from the tracks. Dominique Bordain describes how many residents are asylum seekers and that the encampment cabins are often rented to people who are unaware that evacuation orders have already been issued. Commenting on the cycles of encampment establishment and expulsion, he explains how large-scale settlements evolve in coveted abandoned space, like one known colloquially as Poissonniers (for the rue du Poissonniers, in the 18th arrondissement):

> It's work with no end. We've been at it for years. In terms of securing the space, it is impossible. In terms of managing the spaces, it is clear that it is the usage by neighbours and insertion agencies that helps arrest and contain the phenomenon. The zones that are quasi-systematically abandoned today will be occupied by illicit means. The problem is having zones that are inaccessible, that become unlawful areas. . . . Where we have four families, that's one thing. But we see that if we leave the group alone it's like at Poissonniers

we start with four families, then we have fifty, then we have one hundred. And then we have no idea what to do. So we have to react. . . . Since we have not managed these spaces, in particular the access points, they will never work. Part of our urban planning approach is to turn our backs on the Petite Ceinture, which means that we don't pay attention to open spaces. So these become highly coveted spaces.

Bordain's observations suggest that the hands-off approach by the train company and city not only creates conditions for marginalized groups to seek refuge but also creates conditions that are unacceptable from a social services perspective. His focus on the illicit entry points as the root problem and usage by those who are not homeless as the solution illustrates how inequities are spatialized through regulation of access and occupation. According to this logic, the challenges of homeless encampments are about the wrong people gaining access and using the Petite Ceinture improperly. In the same video, landscape supervisor Lubin Koubaka of Association Espaces (one of the main insertion agencies working on the tracks) shares his frustration in dealing with the continuous cycle of informal settlements, including clearing human waste and refuse. He recounts how repeated vandalism of the workers' access gates to the tracks caused them to simply leave them open, and how his efforts to work with encampment residents by encouraging them to tidy the area with garbage bags were futile, concluding that "There is no solution but to clear out. As long as they are here it will be a rubbish and sewage dump. The Roma need to leave so we can bring in a truck to clear it all up in collaboration with the proprietor." The proprietor, of course, remains the national rail company.

Until 2009, when a 1-km section was opened to the public as the Sentier Nature in the most elite portion of the city, access across the line's 32 km was completely prohibited for humans. Other small stretches have gradually become accessible, with different design approaches and commitments to equity and ecological integrity. But these remain disjointed, like interruptions to the unkempt ribbon of urban wilderness that characterizes the rail line at large. A few prominent stations have been adapted into local food and entertainment hot spots, such as the elegant and upscale *Andia* restaurant in the 16th arrondissement, the hip music and performance venue *La Flêche d'Or* that prioritizes local and marginalized artists in the 20th arrondissement and *La Recyclerie* urban farm, a restaurant and eco-centre in the 18th arrondissement.

Once trains stopped rolling and the SNCF sealed it off, it took a while, almost a decade, before people began venturing in significant numbers to the Petite Ceinture. Even by the mid-2000s, most visitors were either neighbourhood locals walking their dogs or sporadic couples and small groups exploring the old bridges and tunnels. Nonetheless, the stations had attracted human residents for years, even without utilities or easy access into the buildings, as had the sheds and storehouses. Early station colonizers included artistic communities, such as the *Gares aux Gorilles* collective in the northeast portion of the tracks, drawn to the studio-like potential and departure from conventional spatial coding (Foster, 2014). Artists could focus

FIGURE 4.6 La Recyclerie, 2019

Source: Image by J. Foster

on creative exploration without having to budget for Paris' notoriously expensive rental costs. Even before the SNCF ceased operations on the Petite Ceinture, graffiti artists flocked onto the tracks. They could enjoy access to vast surfaces without surveillance and without interruption. They could take their time, work in groups and return to work on pieces for days on end. The stone walls of sunken trenches, columns, tunnel interiors, rail trestles and all corners of the old stations were soon covered in vibrant and colourful graffiti installations. This is one of the most striking features of the Petite Ceinture, perhaps a hallmark of its status as an unrestricted space occupied by those outside the social mainstream. Its unregulated deterioration enabled unregulated creative abundance.

After the freight traffic stopped, the Petite Ceinture quickly became appealing to people participating in subculture activities, like simulated battles or costume performance and play. There were semi-organized events such as dance parties and musical gatherings. Meanwhile, various points along the tracks became reliable spots to acquire and consume illicit drugs beyond the scrutiny of more socially regulated parts of the city. The range of beyond-the-mainstream activities was limitless and often in plain view from the sidewalks surrounding the tracks. There were robberies and assaults, not unlike most spaces of congregation, but for the most part, social groups shared the space peacefully by simply acknowledging one another and keeping a respectful distance.

The tracks also served as relatively discrete locations for sex workers to serve clients. Adjacent to roads and sidewalks, with other sex workers in proximity, the Petite Ceinture offered practical opportunities for those who wanted to remain accessible yet strategically out of sight. It was a great place for outdoor sexual *rendez-vous* in general since the city's parks close at dusk, at which point guards are known to literally chase visitors out before locking gates and patrolling through the night. Many portions of the Petite Ceinture are low-risk settings where locals tend to be sympathetic to, if not unbothered by, queer encounters. The buildings and tunnels offer shelter from elements and/or observation, as well as ease in extracting oneself from the setting. In a densely populated city like Paris, where unsurveilled public space is at a premium, particularly after sundown, the Petite Ceinture offers an urban amenity that thwarts heteronormative environmental order in favour of more open interpretations of what is natural, beautiful and gratifying.

Up to the late 2000s, during the nighttime, only people with a specific purpose ventured onto the tracks. However, during the daylight hours, it became increasingly popular with urban ramblers and naturalists. So popular that it gradually entered the public imagination as a "secret garden" and hidden urban treasure. However rundown buildings or overgrown tracks became, the Petite Ceinture had acquired cache as a charming vestige of yesteryear unbridled by the rest of the city's planning and design regime. Its emergence within the public imagination coincided with the popularity of industrial chic and adaptive reuse of old industrial buildings, such as conversion of warehouses into residential lofts and factories into galleries. But in the case of the Petite Ceinture, things were far grittier and ecologically wilder than in gentrifying working-class neighbourhoods like the Meat Packing District in New York City, so it simply remained an adventurous place to visit rather than adapt and control for capital gain.

By the early 2010s, public interest in the Petite Ceinture was ripening beyond the immediate neighbours. People who lived farther afield, in the central parts of the city as well as visitors to Paris, became aware of this emerging greenspace. It was the subject of a richly illustrated 2003 book entitled *Le Promeneur de la Petite Ceinture* (Chaudun, 2003) that shared the experiences and musings of a six-day journey around the rail line, including reflections on historic legacies, natural succession and human encounters. A 2005 historical account of Paris' rail lines describes the Petite Ceinture as "le plus vaste jardin secret de Paris" (Lamming, 2005, p. 101), and it was also included in a 2005 city guide entitled *Paris Secret* prepared by Paris Musées, the municipal museum agency. The guide is a popular introduction to the city's historic, natural, artistic and architectural features that are less known in the public realm. Still officially prohibited for humans, the guide's synopsis of the Petite Ceinture presents a charming invitation to explore:

> In the breast of France's largest city privileged spaces still exist where nature, almost left to itself, rediscovers part of its entitlements. Forgotten vague terrain, destitute and abandoned gardens, or sites inaccessible to the public form modest reserves, discrete paradises for civic naturalists.

(14)

By the mid-2000s, conditions were well established for artists, squatters, encampment residents, naturalists and recreational visitors. By the late 2000s, human occupation of the Petite Ceinture was becoming more intense, despite fences and signs declaring it off limits. But access was uneven and inequitable around the 32-km perimeter, with some communities embracing inhabitation of the tracks by marginalized Parisians, while other communities actively planned and designed barriers to access for these same groups.

In relation to the encampments, the Petite Ceinture had been appealing to groups of newcomers to Paris long before the media attention of the late 2010s, when the rail company responded to these sites by ejecting residents and demolishing their dwellings, which were often established around station platforms. Residents included migrant groups from eastern Europe, many of whom developed clustered and interconnected structures and set up multi-generational encampments (Foster, 2010). In particular, the visibility of Romani residents along the tracks increased through the 2000s, and their presence inspired considerable debate about the propriety of clandestine communities fully occupying large portions of the tracks. Although they were typically characterized as newcomers, generalizing this entire population as migrants is misleading, since the community within Paris has been established for numerous generations. According to a 2005 report by the European Roma Rights Centre, the vast majority of France's 1.2 million Roma population are French nationals, many of whom regularly experience severe violations of their civil and political rights (ERRC, 2005).

By 2017, the Poissonniers encampment sheltered over 600 people, ranging from infants to seniors. They had established the city's largest *bidonville* (shantytown), in the northern 18th arrondissement. With huts tethered together along the sunken rail verges, circulation was limited to a very narrow footpath lacing the middle of the tracks. Residents created two improvised access points by hacking, grinding and sawing through the iron fence posts and stacking wooden shipping pallets as terraced steps down to the tracks. There were communal toilets and cooking areas, and the expansive encampment was in full view of anyone passing along the surrounding sidewalks and bridges. Media coverage exploded with images of open-air dump piles, vermin as well as children and visibly pregnant residents going about their daily routines among the improvised cabins. By January 2018, the media imagery shifted to the SNCF clearing the entire *bidonville*, with bulldozers dramatically heaping the remnants of people's homes.

The Petite Ceinture provided unique livelihood options for migrants to Paris, particularly those without documentation or access to social services and affordable housing. But many of the people living on the Petite Ceinture in the two decades after freight traffic ceased were not newcomers to Paris. For these long-time residents of Paris, the rail line offered a viable way to exist in the city. As a linear yet isolated landmass inset within the city, homeless people could access paid employment and social services and make use of livelihood resources such as gathering food or staying connected with social networks and family. Police seldom ventured onto the Petite Ceinture, and neighbours didn't tend to pay attention to what was happening, so long as lodgings were relatively concealed, litter didn't accumulate and noisy disturbances were minimized. The problem was not that people ventured onto the tracks. That had been going on for decades. Nor was it that people were engaging in illegal activities (also commonplace for decades). It wasn't even the act of living full-time on the tracks, since homeless residents had long been tolerated. Rather, it was largely the fact that this was a Roma-identified community, and they were, taking up space collectively in ways that breach Western conventions of decorum. This was not the ideal of a green network filled with convivial opportunities appealing to diverse publics that was envisioned in the 2013 public consultation process. Roma people are systemically marginalized targets of environmental injustice across Europe (Environmental Justice Atlas, 2022), with a long history of displacement from greenspaces and areas with life-sustaining resources, especially when these areas are economically valued (Heidegger & Wiese, 2020). However, the removal of the encampments is rationalized (including in the name of biodiversity conservation), and evictions from the Petite Ceinture are most certainly aligned with the long and deep legacy of Roma displacement. Inclusivity and freedom to inhabit the Petite Ceinture are clearly not limitless, and in this instance, enforcement of those limits was experienced by a historically oppressed community.

Unambiguously uneven terrain

It is remarkable that such a rich and vast ecological asset could be quickly established in a densely settled city like Paris. For most cities seeking to enhance their network of green spaces, this is an unimaginable dream come true. What makes the Petite Ceinture even more interesting is that it crosses through so many neighbourhoods. Parisian topography is highly varied, and this is dealt with by means of tunnels, bridges and trestles to ensure a continuous pathway at a steady elevation. But neighbourhood variations in socio-economic conditions have not been engineered to a level standard, and the Petite Ceinture traverses the city's extremes. Although the city is topographically and socio-economically uneven, the 32-km circuit of the Petite Ceinture weaves a continuous and level ecological corridor.

In the west, the line travels through Paris' elite 16th arrondissement, well known for lavish homes, posh stores and exclusive social clubs. Residents tend to be proprietors of their homes, and this arrondissement has minimal social housing (APUR, 2016). In contrast, the northeast arrondissements (the 18th, 19th and 20th) are the city's industrial heartland. These neighbourhoods are more populated by working-class communities and new immigrants, many of whom live in towers along the Petite Ceinture's outer edges. Locals often have a direct labour connection to the rail line's industrial heritage. These communities are characterized by higher proportions of single-parent families living in public housing complexes, supported by social assistance, especially right along the edges of the Petite Ceinture (APUR, 2016). The city's median household income levels are highest in the centre, south and west, with the wealthiest neighbourhoods right along the western stretches of the Petite Ceinture. Meanwhile, the city's poorest neighbourhoods are concentrated at the north and eastern edges of the rail line (APUR, 2015). Analysis of changes between 2001 and 2016 suggests that this pattern has only intensified through the first part of the 21st century (APUR, 2017). On the outside of the Petite Ceinture, in Paris' suburbs, the pattern amplifies, with communities in the north and east historically and currently in the lowest income quintiles, while those in the west remain in the top quintile (APUR, 2020). The city's planning department summarizes this tenacious pattern of spatialized inequality as "confirming major trends inherited from the past" and affirms that "In the face of this result that is not new and seems to be augmenting, the goal of territorial rebalancing remains to prioritize, at a minimum, access to the same levels of services and amenities for all urban residents" (APUR, 2020, p. 20).

Urban landscapes are socially differentiated through decisions to invest in, create and nurture ecological spaces. A comparative study of the "naturalization" of two decommissioned rail lines, New York City's High Line and Paris' Petite Ceinture, probes how this is amplified with the "rediscovery" of post-industrial lands (Foster, 2010). In each case, ecological enhancement serves as an instrument of social order, producing subjectivities that distinguish those entitled to use the space and clarify who is unwelcome. When ecological investment into the Petite Ceinture commenced, it was in response to security concerns, and it was in the 16th arrondissement. Although ecological conditions in this stretch were not particularly distinct from any other portions of the rail line, the decision to prioritize securitization and ecological enhancement of this specific part of the 32-km loop sprung from neighbourhood resistance to alternatives planned by the SNCF, such as a parking garage. Elite neighbours successfully lobbied in favour of a nature path, even though the community is adjacent to the Bois de Boulogne and is replete with gardens and parks. Workers with the insertion agency Association Espaces worked diligently for six years to transform the 1.5-km section by removing the tracks, clearing and then replacing trees and shrubs and importing new soil and mulch. They created six distinct ecozones (a prairie, a humid zone, a meadow, a wooded zone, a transition zone and a wildflower zone) and translated the City's park design into reality. The space was officially opened in 2007 as the Sentier Nature and the city purchased it from the rail company in 2009, an exception to the SNCF retention policy that was not permitted or sought elsewhere along the line.

This is one of Paris' *beaux quartiers* (beautiful neighbourhoods), and in addition to resisting a parking garage, the local residents also rejected the aesthetic composition of the space as *terrains vague* or *délaissé urbain*. Unlike the rest of the Petite Ceinture, the segment was no longer a novel ecosystem but rather corresponds with Higgs' (2017) typologies for hybrid or designed ecosystems. The degree of intervention is heavy, but ongoing management is low to moderate. Historicity is low, with few indications of any industrial heritage, aside from the linear formation and a renovated station. Management interventions at the Sentier Nature, meanwhile, are ecosystem-centred in terms of the biophysical attributes but human-centred in terms of securing the space from undesirable people and uses. It is a regulated space that reflects clear management ideals, without any of the decay that characterizes

FIGURE 4.7   Sentier Nature, Petite Ceinture 16th arrondissement, 2019

Source: Image by J. Foster

the rest of the rail line. It is not a manicured park, but there is no mistaking the Sentier Nature for an urban void or abandoned space. In this way, it is ecologically and aesthetically distinct from the rest of the Petite Ceinture. There is no trash, it is carefully landscaped, and surrounding noises are buffered. Soft mulch is underfoot, and there are no foul odours or perilous obstructions. It is serene and uncrowded, with comfortable benches and structures upon which to rest and commune. There are no signs of urban blight and certainly no encampments. Rather, there is educational signage about the ecological communities, carefully arranged log piles and the old train station at the northern end has been reconfigured into a stylish restaurant with picture windows and a terrace overlooking the path. Most visitors are local dog walkers or leisurely strollers. Entrances to the parc, like other parks in Paris, are locked each night. The attributes of *terrain vague* that open opportunities for enhancing environmental justice, such as alternatives to mainstream ideals and affiliations, are simply scrubbed out of the Sentier Nature. The space has been composed to limit access, under the cloak of ecological benevolence, and to instil social order in response to the preferences of the most socio-economically privileged Parisians.

Another portion of the Petite Ceinture has undergone a similar fate, albeit one that is ecologically unfavourable. Transformation of 1.3 km in the 15th arrondissement into a public trail has received very mixed reviews. On the one hand, the

FIGURE 4.8 Petite Ceinture, 15th arrondissement, 2017

Source: Image by J. Foster

City opened the space with universal access standards, including elevators, smooth composite surfacing and wide open sight lines. On the other hand, all vegetation was removed to create a clear corridor denuded of plants and wildlife. This does not correspond with the goals of the Paris Environmental Health Plan (Mairie de Paris, 2015b), Adaptation Strategy (Mairie de Paris, 2015a) or Climate Action Plan

(Mairie de Paris, 2018b) for a carbon neutral city, much less the target of 40% permeable greenspace set in the City's 2018–24 Biodiversity Plan. It was received with derision by environmentally concerned Parisians. Over time, with strong restraint of ongoing management, plants and animals have returned, particularly those travelling between the parc André-Citroën (a former car factory) and parc Georges-Brassens (a former abattoir).

Temporary urbanism

The planning approach that the City adopts for the Petite Ceinture is oriented around impermanence. Everything, aside from the Sentier Nature in the 16th arrondissement, is an interim use. This approach is characterized by Emanuelle Roux, Architect-Planner for the City's Planning Agency APUR, as "temporary urbanism." It is in part a response to the SNCF dictates around reclaiming the line at an unspecified point in the future and the concurrent requirement that the tracks stay clear. Roux (2017) explains that this entails monitoring and preserving a "memory" of the evolution of the rail line, maintaining the "global identity" of the Petite Ceinture, thinking about the role of the line in relation to commitments to enhance nature in the city and, whenever possible, creating new usages for the city's residents. She recounts how "we have to keep the memory and the unity of the place without forbidding a better future for it and something shared smartly. It is a new form of urban planning which is temporary urbanism."

The City of Paris recently declared its allegiance to temporary urbanism as a means of adding value to so-called vacant space. The phenomenon of interim, episodic uses of spaces perceived to be abandoned, derelict or simply underused has flooded cities across Europe and North America over the past two decades (Latham, 2018; Madanipour, 2018). For instance, unoccupied storefronts might host "pop-up" retail events, empty warehouses might be transformed into performance space or a community garden might be planted along a hydro-corridor. Projects, installations and events are short-term and ephemeral, not planned as permanent engagements. This is an institutional approach that is distinct from the clandestine and underground leisure, cultural, exploratory and livelihood activities that often thrive in post-industrial spaces [see Edensor (2005), Anguelovski (2014) and Hou (2010)]. Champions of temporary urbanism celebrate these as opportunities for adaptive re-uses that are creative and engaging. Breitbart (2013), for instance, points out that

> Temporary occupations of everyday space and innovative designs prioritize critical dialogue about how space is used over new construction. They can also promote a more subversive and often aesthetic experimentation with land use as decisions are made about the re-purposing of vacant and underutilized land.
>
> *(289)*

Critics, meanwhile, decry them as precursors to gentrification, as neoliberal instruments to financialize under-performing sites through "creative city" strategies, and as cooptive of grassroots organizational systems (Bragaglia & Rossingolo, 2021). Temporary urbanism is now an official policy in Paris. In August 2019, the City signed a charter with property owners (private and public, including SNCF) and real estate developers, an agreement that derives from pilot projects like Les Cinq Toits in the 16th arrondissement, a 27-month conversion of a former police barracks into shelter for refugees and families. Presumably, the massive bentonite processing facility is an applied example of temporary urbanism.

The approach is deeper than just adherence to edicts and regulations, and it takes in an obligation to equity, as well as limitations of knowledge about what is best in evolving urban spaces. In greenspaces, the foundation of temporary urbanism is also rooted in appreciation for *terrains vague*. Speaking in 2011, former Deputy Mayor Fabienne Giboudeaux, charged with the city's green spaces, centres the needs of residents in the northern and eastern arrondissements, where people have fewer outdoor spaces, less leisure time and less ability to travel. Her reasoning for not proceeding with the permanent development of untended and ostensibly vacant spaces embraces self-sustaining indeterminacy as a valuable socio-ecological asset. She is most mindful of youth demands for unmanicured greenspace:

> I think we need to tell planners to leave *terrains vague*. For several reasons. Because these are spaces where nature exists spontaneously, so it is always interesting to see what happens. Because these are spaces where we do not intervene, where humans are less present, so there is a lifesystem that is interesting in terms of biodiversity. And to leave the possibility for projects we have not yet contemplated. Planners always want to fill space when they present plans, and people are anxious. They say "Ah, but what will happen? We are going to leave the space as is?" I think we need to educate people a bit to explain that yes, it's interesting because these spaces might not have value for us, but they have strong economic value and value for birds, they need space that is not heavily used, and also tell them that uses and needs evolve and we need to leave space for that.

There is tension between competing perspectives on ecological valuation within temporary urbanism. This comes down to a disagreement between the "let it be" approach of the *terrains vague* or *délaissé urbain* perspective and the desire for ongoing management and utilization of the space for gardening and other human benefits. On the Petite Ceinture, for instance, should the wild novel ecological systems that gave rise to 32 km of ecological continuity and biodiversity be prioritized, or should opportunities for residents to cultivate and manipulate the landscape be given precedence? As noted in the 2013 public consultations, although there was an overall endorsement for open-air *espace de respiration* and the environmental qualities of the Petite Ceinture, perspectives on the appropriate form, function and design approach differed greatly. Going back to 2011, Prochasson notes that on the Petite Ceinture, "we often talk about playgrounds and shared gardens, which is a way to conquer the spaces because the city is very dense." He interprets this friction in the eastern portion of the line by explaining:

> The development of organic food is linked to the idea that nature is evolving in the wrong way, that people want to find more ecological options. For example, the trend is to install hives in the city as reaction to information about bees being endangered by pesticides and the desire for better food. There is a general reaction to ask for more natural spaces in urban developments, and to have more natural food. In the 20th arrondissement we cannot reclaim space. If a shared garden is established on the station quay where nothing grows it has no impact. But if we transform natural space, like in the shared gardens between two tunnels in the 20th, we completely change the environment. There is a contradictory demand from inhabitants who want shared gardens and those who want biodiversity. The biggest challenge is not to plan, it is to impede efforts to plan for the Petite Ceinture. We have said that we will not plan, we'll open. We will open, we will test, we will construct things, and we will see what happens. . . . We will not begin by designing, we will begin by opening. We will see afterwards what we need to design. The only planning that happened was in sequences to see what we would open and when and how, so it could be equitable between the different arrondissements.
>
> *(Blancot, 2017)*

The state rail company remains proprietor, and decisions about the rail line's future ultimately lie with its administration. The commitment to preserve the possibility of train resumption may seem unrealistic, and it may even seem disingenuous in light of some of the conversions that have been executed. Within this context, the ability of planners, elected officials, neighbours and fans of the Petite Ceinture to rationalize unplanning is remarkable. Leaving most of it as is, letting it run fallow and wild amid the intensity of neoliberal capital urbanization, has allowed space for critical socio-ecological relationships that could never be designed or otherwise even imagined. These spaces are urban sustainability success stories, at least for as long as the rail line obliges.

Bibliography

Anguelovski, I. (2014). *Neighborhood as refuge: Community reconstruction, place remaking, and environmental justice in the city*. The MIT Press.

Atelier Parisien d'Urbanism (APUR). (2011). *Situation et Perspectives de La Place de La Nature à Paris: 3e Atelier – La Petite Ceinture Ferroviaire*. Author.

Atelier Parisien d'Urbanism (APUR). (2015). *Caractérisation Des Quartiers Selon Le Niveau de Revenu Des Habitants*. Author.

Atelier Parisien d'Urbanism (APUR). (2016). *Caractérisation Des Quartiers En Fonction Du Profil Socio-Économique Surreprésenté*. Author.

Atelier Parisien d'Urbanism (APUR). (2017). *Revenu Médian Déclaré : Évolution de l'écart à La Médiane Parisienne Entre 2001 et 2016 à Paris.* Author.

Atelier Parisien d'Urbanism (APUR). (2020). *Évolutions Des Revenus Dans La Métropole Du Grand Paris.* Author.

Blancot, C. (2017, April 24). Personal communication.

Bragaglia, F., & Rossignolo, C. (2021). Temporary urbanism as a new policy strategy: A contemporary panacea or a Trojan horse? *International Planning Studies, 26*(4), 370–386.

Breitbart, M. M. (2013). Afterword: Moving towards 'creative sustainability' in post-industrial communities. In M. M. Breitbart (Ed.), *Creative economies in post-industrial cities: Manufacturing a (different) scene* (pp. 277–310). Routledge.

Bretelle, B. (2015, November 14). Brief history of the Petite Ceinture Circular Railway of Paris. *Association Sauvegarde Petite Ceinture.* www.petiteceinture.org/Brief-history-of-the-Petite-Ceinture-circular-railway-of-Paris.html.

Brun, M., Di Pietro, F., & Bonthoux, S. (2017). Residents' perceptions and valuations of urban wastelands are influenced by vegetation structure. *Urban Forestry and Urban Greening, 29,* 393–403.

Chaudun, N. (2003). *Le Promeneur De La Petite Ceinture: Récit De Voyage.* Actes sud, Paris Musées.

Contassot, Y. (2017, December 3). *Le massacre de la Petite Ceinture dans le 13è arrondissement.* https://yvescontassot.eu/?p=7357.

Edensor, T. (2005). *Industrial ruins: Space, aesthetics and materiality.* Berg.

Environmental Justice Atlas. Pushed to the wasteland: Environmental racism against Roma Communities in Central and South-Eastern Europe. *Environmental Justice Atlas.* Retrieved January 26, 2022, from https://ejatlas.org/featured/roma.

European Roma Rights Centre. (2005, November). *Always somewhere else: Anti-gypsyism in France.* Country Report Series No. 15.

Feredj, R. (2016, May 3). RATP's real estate enhancement policy in Paris. *Intelligent Transport.* https://www.intelligenttransport.com/transport-articles/19088/ratp-real-estate-enhancement-policy-paris/.

Foster, J. (2010). Off track, in nature: Constructing ecology on old rail lines in Paris and New York. *Nature and Culture, 5*(3), 316–337.

Foster, J. (2014). Hiding in plain view: Vacancy and prospect in Paris' Petite Ceinture. *Cities, 40*(B): 124–132.

Godard, F. (2017a). *Biodiversité en Danger sur la Petite Ceinture.* www.youtube.com/watch?v=AygIk_piDxU.

Godard, F. (2017b). *La Petite Ceinture Refuge.* www.youtube.com/watch?v=sLcKaB2aigE.

Godard, F. (2019). *De la Jungle au Jardin des Traverses sur la Petite Ceinture – Paris 18e.* www.youtube.com/watch?v=9YcZb32sE-A.

Gouyette, B. (2017, April 28). Personal communication.

Heidegger, P., & Wiese, K. (2020). *Pushed to the wastelands: Environmental racism against Roma Communities in Central and Eastern Europe.* European Environmental Bureau.

Higgs, E. (2017). Novel and designed ecosystems. *Restoration Ecology, 25*(1), 8–13.

Hou, J. (2010). *Insurgent public space: Guerilla urbanism and the remaking of contemporary cities.* Routledge.

Japiot, X., & du Plessis. A. (2017). *Étude des services écologiques rendus par la Petite Ceinture ferroviaire de Paris: Biodiversité et continuités écologiques.* Marie de Paris (Agence d'écologie urbaine), SNCF Réseau.

Lamming, C. (2005). *Paris Ferroviaire.* Editions Parigramme.

Latham, L. (2018, November 28). The rise of 'meanwhile space': How empty properties are finding second lives. *The Guardian,* sec. Cities. www.theguardian.com/cities/2018/nov/28/the-rise-of-the-meanwhile-space-how-empty-properties-are-finding-second-lives.

Lindo, D. (2015). Tales from the concrete jungle: Urban birding around the world. Bloomsbury.

Madanipour, A. (2018). Temporary us of space: Urban processes between flexibility, opportunity and precarity. *Urban Studies, 55*(5), 1093–1110.

Mairie de Paris. (2011). *Plan Biodiversité de Paris – Programme d'actions pour préserver et enrichir la biodiversité à Paris.* Direction des Espaces Verts et de l'Environnement, Agence d'écologie urbaine.

Mairie de Paris. (2015a). *Paris's adaptation strategy: Towards a more resilient city.*

Mairie de Paris. (2015b). *Plan Parisien de Santé Environnementale: Tous ensemble pour une ville-santé.*

Mairie de Paris. (2018a). *Plan de biodiversité de Paris 2018–2024.*

Mairie de Paris. (2018b). *Plan climat de Paris: Vers une ville neutre en canbone, 100% énergies renouvelebles, résiliente, juste et inclusive.*

Mairie de Paris et Réseau ferré de France (RFF). (2013). *Bilan de la concertation sur l'avenir de la Petite Ceinture, 27 décembre 2012–14 février 2013.*

Mairie de Paris et Réseau ferré de France (RFF). (2015). *Protocole-cadre entre la Ville de Paris et la group SNCF concernant le devenir de la Petite Ceinture ferroviaire à Paris.*

Mairie de Paris and SNCF. (2017). *Étude des services écologiques rendus par la Petite Ceinture ferroviaire de Paris.*

Menant, P.-A. (2017). *La Petite Ceinture de Paris et La Ligne d'Auteuil.* Éditions du Petit Pavé.

O'Sullivan, F. (2016, July 26). A high line for Paris, only more so: The transformation of the Petite Ceinture will ultimately become the city's biggest-ever railway conversion project. *Bloomberg.Com.* www.bloomberg.com/news/articles/2016-07-26/in-paris-railway-conversions-like-the-petite-ceinture-are-suddenly-everywhere.

Préfet de la Région d'Île-de-France. (2013). *Schéma Régional de Cohérence Ecologique de la région Île-de-France.*

Préfet de la Région d'Île-de-France. (2017a). *Plan régional d'actions en faveur des chiroptères en Île-de-France 2012–2016.* Direction Régionale et Interdépartementale de l'Environment et de l'Énergie.

Préfet de la Région d'Île-de-France. (2017b). *Plan Vert de l'Île-de-France: La nature pour tous et partout.*

Prochasson, M. (2011). Personal communication.

Réseau ferrée de France (RFF). (2006). *Mairie de Paris. Protocol-cadre entre la Ville de Paris et Réseau ferrée de France concernant la petite ceinture à Paris.*

Roux, E. (2017). Personal communication.

Saito, Y. (1998). The aesthetics of unscenic nature. *The Journal of Aesthetics and Art Criticism, 56*(2), 101–111.

Société nationale des chemins de fer français (SNCF). (2016). *Dix ans chantiers d'insertion: Entretien de la Petite Ceinture.*

Société nationale des chemins de fer français (SNCF), Mairie de Paris. (2015). *Protocol-cadre entre la Ville de Paris et le group SNCF concernant le devenir de la petite ceinture ferroviaire à Paris.*

Strohmayer, U., and Corre, J. (2012). Performing marginal space: Film, topology and the Petite Ceinture in Paris. *Liminalities: A Journal of Performance Studies, 8*(4), 1–16.

Terrier, J.-E., & Delziani, S. (2018). *La Saga de La Petite Ceinture, 1997–2017 Tome II.* Éditions de la Vie du Rail.

5

THE LESLIE STREET SPIT

Toronto, Canada

The cases explored in this book share a legacy of being developed for industrial usages that were once central to their local civic fabric. Whether it was manufacturing or freight transportation, as in Milwaukee's Menomonee Valley and Paris' Petite Ceinture, or any of the varied transformations from industrial to greenspace in Honolulu, Berlin or The Bronx, what each location shares is a history of robust industrial activity that supported thousands of livelihoods and shaped urban economies. In each case, a pattern emerges: disengagement of industrial infrastructure from the momentum of urban growth, a period of biophysical neglect and managerial indeterminacy and succession into novel ecological and social formations. Cessation of industrial activities opened new socio-ecological opportunities and, in each case, the sites emerged from both pre-industrial and industrial functions as altogether distinct landscapes.

What sets Toronto's Leslie Street Spit apart is that all of this happened in the midst of industrial activity, while the site was being actively used and altered on a weekly basis as a dump. As a celebrated "feral" greenspace that co-existed with industrial activity, the Leslie Street Spit – commonly known as the Spit – functions in Toronto's civic popular imagination as a beloved counterpoint to the ecologically destructive effects of contemporary urban development. It is vibrant in the midst of despoliation, with critical habitat springing from the city's refuse. Birds nest among the smashed remains, verdant greenery roots into the rubble, and mid-sized mammals comingle with heavy machinery. It helps heighten appreciation of urban ecology and novel urban ecosystems with constant pulses of new species and changes to habitat composition. Celebration of the Spit also produces specific stories about the world, and these stories are politically charged. As a "happy accident" that transformed industrial ruin into wilderness, it performs some political heavy lifting by naturalizing the material connections between the demolition of actual urban communities and greenspace production. It also obscures ways that

DOI: 10.4324/9781315106403-5

wildlife is imperilled by exposure to urban hazards. Finally, sustaining the habitat conditions that triggered the Spit's protection as feral greenspace requires continual management, which is dependent on urban economic growth. The Leslie Street Spit animates the dynamics of creative destruction as a core process in the formation of contemporary cities, and it does so in ways that are rarely acknowledged in academic research and thought.

The Spit is a 5-km-long construction waste dump in the heart of Toronto. It juts straight southward from the city's central shoreline into Lake Ontario, forming a linear and vibrant ecological refuge for an astounding array of flora and fauna. It is a human-induced landform, constructed out of landfill and port dredgeate, that has also become a world-class birding site. The Spit is a relatively new landform, initiated only in 1959. It was envisioned as a means to simultaneously shelter the city's downtown harbour, create the conditions to welcome an aspirational shipping industry and discard the detritus of the city's building boom. Its ecological richness was unforeseen. Rather, it sprung from spontaneous invasion by birds stopping over to rest during their yearly migration back and forth across the lake. The seeds and biomass that birds dropped in their guano propagated plants that spawned more seeds and more biomass. This combined with potential seedbed from the silty dredgeate extracted from the city's inner harbour, as well as seeds conceivably blown downwind from the nearby Toronto Islands. Over years, soil

FIGURE 5.1 Leslie Street Spit meadow rubble pile, 2020

Source: Image by J. Foster

gradually built up to the point where the evolving dump became a major hot spot for birds in the Great Lakes. It wasn't long before the birds built nests and established colonies amid the dump trucks and piles of new detritus. While some treated it merely as a convenient stop-over, there was no mistaking the allure of the space for those seeking a foothold in the city. Ring-billed gulls (*Laurus elawarensips*) were early colonizers and provide a vivid illustration of the Spit's appeal to migrating birds. Their population rose from 21 pairs in 1973 to over 70,000 pairs by 1981 (Foster & Sandberg, 2004). By 2000, the ring-bill gull population had surged to the point where it comprised 6% of the world's breeding population, all nesting on a few of the Spit's narrow peninsulas. Also notable were the colonies of herring gull (*Laurus argentatus*), common tern (*Sterna hirundo*), double-crested cormorant (*Phalacrocorax auratus*) and as much as 30% of Canada's population of black-crown night-heron (*Nycticorax nycicorax*) (TRCA, 2000).

This is an impressive concentration of bird habitat for any major city, even more so considering the site's location in the city's central industrial heart. The tight layering of the nesting colonies has developed into a three-dimensional puzzle, creating an ecologically unique community structure without any unclaimed space. But what is truly striking is that this ecological jewel evolved out of waste in the midst of persistent industrial activity. In a 2020 episode of the television documentary program *The Nature of Things* entitled "Accidental Wilderness," wildlife ecologist Gail Fraser excavates an empty cormorant nest to demonstrate the unusual habitat composition. She uncovers metal wire, stiff synthetic strapping tape, insulated wires, clothing and personal effects, plastic implements and sundry garbage. Fraser explains, "usually, their nests are made out of sticks, but they're also just taking stuff that's in their environment," which is borne from "a history of being made out of human-made materials . . . this stuff never goes away."

The biophysical history of the Spit is compelling, given its function as a repository of the city's unwanted materials. Best known and most clearly visible among these are construction products that can be easily discerned as bricks and building objects. But the material composition of the landmass is far more complex than the official description "construction waste" suggests. All that is discarded is not necessarily unwanted or expired, and this is where environmental justice concerns emerge. Despite the oft-repeated characterization of the base materials as "clean fill," the Spit is also composed of homes and neighbourhoods that, at some point, were considered undesirable. The demolition of particular communities and their disposal at the edge of the city cast a more socially poignant historical read on the Leslie Street Spit. In this way, the Spit also functions as an urban socio-political archive. And the fact that these communities' stories have been buried by the combined narratives of "clean fill" and "urban wilderness oasis" is a testament to the power of ecology to distract from unjust and inequitable urban ideals in the name of neoliberal progress. What's more, it underscores both the appeal and limitations of the popular narrative that nature can heal the scars of the past.

This chapter takes up the case of Toronto's Leslie Street Spit and affirms its critical function as an alternative to conventional urban greenspace, both socially and ecologically. In doing so, the chapter also troubles the notions of ecological remedy to urban destruction and points to some blind spots in the celebratory narratives of post-industrial urban greenspace.

When a dump becomes a refuge

With its stratified layers of detritus and ecological vibrancy, the Leslie Street Spit presents a fascinating urban prototype. From an ecological perspective, it has evolved as *terrain vague*. With indeterminate and unbounded possibilities, the stage is set for ecological succession to proceed in unexpected ways. As a novel ecosystem, habitat design was not a consideration until it was compelled by environmental conservation designations. Novel ecological combinations are expressions of adaptation to urban settlement. Animals learn to eat and acquire foods that are readily available, adjust their circadian rhythms to increased light exposure and metabolize urban-abundant minerals like the salts on roadways and fast foods. They adapt their ranges and techniques for sheltering their offspring. Plants that take up concentrated contaminants (like mercury, lead and cadmium) thrive alongside species that can self-fertilize in fragmented habitats without pollinators. Species that co-habitate are either tolerant of or adapted to ambient, low-frequency noise, hotter microclimates and reduced genetic variation. At the Leslie Street Spit, we find the four major urban filters that Williams et al. (2009) propose as a conceptual framework for understanding ecological responses to urbanization: habitat transformation, fragmentation, urban environs and human preferences. Contrary to the cynicism that often accompanies reputedly destroyed sites, in the case of the Leslie Street, Spit these provide the conditions that prompt the exceptional successional processes driving the formulation of novel ecosystems.

As a present-day dump and part of a protective reef around the city's harbour, the Spit is also clearly part of the logic of urban development and capital accumulation. Through this legacy, it carries a material record of the succession of the city's built environment. Base minerals at the Spit originated hundreds of kilometres away in pits and quarries on the escarpment and moraine beyond the outskirts of the city. They were then transformed into the bricks, blocks and cement that composed Toronto's built structures. When these buildings were demolished and replaced, the minerals were finally laid to rest as fill that expands the city's southern boundaries into the lake. They form the substrate for the novel ecological assemblages that self-organized. Urbanized capitalism depends on a cycle of extraction, recomposition, building, demolition and disposal. This continuous loop is an expression of the economic rationale of creative destruction as a means to reaccumulate wealth by devaluing and annihilating existing structures. Where the capabilities of buildings to function as economic assets are unsatisfactory for wealth accumulation, capitalism responds with a "spatial fix" in the form of creative destruction, presenting new opportunities to absorb surplus capital, increase production and expand profits (Harvey, 2001). But the materials at the Spit also carry an archival record of dispossession that is perhaps less well known and raises important questions about whose

FIGURE 5.2 Aerial image (n–n–e) of Leslie Street Spit, Toronto Port Lands and downtown Toronto, 2019

Source: Image by J. Foster

buildings were devalued and annihilated, and whose histories are acknowledged
in official and popular accounts of urban renewal, even when it produces critical
habitat out of the recombinant landscape.

The stunning combinations of post-industrial waste, verdant greens, abundant
wildlife and open skyline are certainly intriguing. They have transformed the Spit
into a beloved "accidental wilderness" that is fiercely protected from development
by legions of nature lovers and recreationists. Yet, however remarkable this amalga-
mation is, it also conceals stories of social marginalization and community destruction that are intrinsic parts of the city's evolution. Furthermore, since it is a dump
that absorbs a range of materials, including toxic waste, to furnish an ecological
refuge amid the dense urban fabric, the Spit raises important questions about the
ethics of creating habitat that attracts fauna and exposes animals to contaminants
and perilous landscape features. As materials accumulate, they are metabolized by
the non-human bodies that inhabit the Spit, presenting serious new harm. And as

animals make use of the wider landscape surroundings, such as the harbour and network of green corridors lacing the city, they are exposed to new risks.

For over 50 years, dump trucks rumbled onto the Spit on weekdays, passing through the weigh station where waste materials were inspected and drivers received instructions about where to discard their spoils. These spoils formed the landscape substrate, combining rebar, chunks of cement sidewalks, porcelain, bricks, broken telephone poles, ceramic tiling, building foundations and whatever other structural elements were demolished and discarded. Journalist Stephen Marche (2010) describes the Leslie Street Spit as "the most attractive dump in the world, a taste of what the posthuman world would look like." While trucks were rolling in, birds were also building nests on the ground, in the trees and along the shoreline. The dump trucks and the birds co-existed, and each year, the overall area of the Spit would expand further off the shore and deeper into the lake. It wasn't long before the Spit functioned simultaneously as an operative dump and a nature oasis.

The overall landscape is composed of narrow roadways roughly forming an obtuse triangle. Early dumping created the central spine, which supports the longest side of the triangle. Facing north-westward towards the city, with a series of parallel narrow peninsulas that protect embayments, this side also features an inlet that opens into three retention ponds at the centre of the Spit. The inlet is a passageway for barges to enter and deposit silt and materials dredged from the city's Don River. Given the tenets of the Great Lake Water Quality Agreement, which forbid dumping dredgeate into open water, the Leslie Street Spit has become the final resting place for the toxins, heavy metals and detritus that accumulate through the Don Watershed (which covers about half the city) and harbour. The southeastern side of the Spit is a straight, narrow causeway of about 4 km that absorbs most of the wave action from Lake Ontario. At the northern end, where an inactive lighthouse is perched upon a hill, the skyline is a wide open lake. Dump trucks almost completely stopped disposing of waste in 2019, so large-scale landscape supplementation efforts are now complete. But they continue dumping along the southeastern shoreline and will likely do so in perpetuity, as a means of fortifying the narrow landmass in response to constant erosion from lake waves.

The Leslie Street Spit didn't start out as an urban wilderness gem. In fact, its current ecological attributes weren't even imagined as part of its function or character. In the 1950s, when the Toronto Port Authority envisioned a simple breakwater to protect the city's harbour and port lands, there were no plans whatsoever for any type of covering. It was simply a spot to dump materials and leave them exposed to the elements, a mere scrapyard that could conveniently serve as a physical barrier while extending the city's property line into the lake. Early dumping developed as an extension of the city's Port Lands. It formed what is now known as the Spit's baselands, the part closest to the city that is not surrounded by water. At this point, it was a straightforward lakeshore perimeter extension, without discernible projection into the lake. Dumping served to infill the remnants of one of eastern Canada's largest wetlands, Ashbridges Bay. According to the Don River

Historical Mapping Project, this area was heavily contaminated by Toronto's earlier industrial activities, such as the Gooderham & Worts distillery and cattle byres (Bonnel, 2009). Infill was part of the Ashbridges Bay Reclamation Scheme, coordinated by the Toronto Harbour Commission to drain the marsh in order to create new port land and industrial terrain. By the 1970s, major industrial activities included the Hearn Generating Station (which supplied electricity for much of the city) and the Ashbridges Bay Wastewater Treatment Plant. Petroleum refining and storage, equipment manufacturing, steel foundries, liquid and solid waste management, vehicle maintenance and repair operations and municipal services such as incineration are but a sample of the diverse heavy industrial uses of the Port Lands that flourished from the 1970s onward (SLR Consulting Canada Ltd, 2009). A 2016 environmental report identifies 28 potentially contaminating activities in the Port Lands, including coal gasification, rubber manufacturing, explosives and munitions manufacturing, iron and steel production, metal treatment and fabrication and crude oil refining (CH2M Hill Canada Ltd., 2016).

The landform began jutting southward straight into the lake in the mid-1960s, developing into a promontory known as Spine Road that was the Spit's preliminary geomorphological composition. Vegetation remained scarce through the mid-1970s, and the surface was dominated by smashed construction materials and silt from the inner harbour. The Spit was officially inaccessible to humans, with no trails or non-industrial access points. People mostly knew about it by word of mouth. In 1973, the Toronto Harbour Commission sanctioned civilian visits to the Spit in the form of organized bus tours on Sundays (attended by 2,300 people that year), and the following year allowed cyclists and pedestrians to access the Spit independently (Carley, 2022). It was only open to the public on weekends between June and September, when the western half became a park managed by the Toronto and Region Conservation Authority (TRCA). The active dumping along the southeast portion continued, and this area remained off limits to recreational visitors.

It wasn't until the late 1970s when the Metro Toronto and Region Conservation Authority (MTRCA, now TRCA) was assigned to develop a master plan for an aquatic park that the value of the Spit as an ecological and recreational amenity began to hit the public radar. By this point, birds had already found the Spit and were forming massive colonies. Local birdwatchers were taking note. The earliest stages of vegetation succession brought Scouring rush (*Equisetum hyemale*), Redosier dogwood (*Cornus stolonifera*) and other hardy species rooting into the rubble. Before long, the western half of the Spit was green with stands of trembling aspen. By the early 1980s, it was a veritable greenspace in the city, and human visitors were frequenting on a regular basis.

The Spit quickly became established as an off-the-beaten-track destination that was proximate to downtown. It was a spot where people could detach from the conventional urban experience and commune with nature, find solitude or simply enjoy a change of scenery. Although it is difficult to estimate the exact number of people who visited the Spit at this point, it is easy to ascertain that for many the Spit had already become a beloved urban idiosyncrasy, something unique and unexpected in a drab city like Toronto that was not known for eccentricities. And as more and more birds flocked in, so did the serious bird enthusiasts. Before long, it became a hot spot on the birding scene, especially during the spring migration. In 1982, bird nesting and breeding in the verdant north-west portion of the Spit inspired designation as a provincially Environmentally Significant Area (ESA), and in 2000, it was declared a Globally Significant Important Bird Area by BirdLife International. Although the variety and population sizes of birds shifted dramatically each year, there was no doubt that it was one of the most dynamic and accessible spots for bird enthusiasts, including everyone from amateur hobbyists to expert ornithologists.

The impressive representation of birds may have attracted the most public ecological appreciation of the Leslie Street Spit, but there were other reasons to celebrate the landform's natural attributes. Shorebirds, songbirds and raptors shared the Spit with an extraordinary array of butterflies, reptiles and amphibians. Leagues of Eastern cottontail rabbit (*Sylvilagus floridanus*) populated the Spit, and coyotes (*Canis latrans*) and red fox (*Vulpes vulpes*) established permanent dens, while other mammals feasted on the ground nests. What's more, the evolution of vegetation presented an incredible living laboratory of urban succession processes. By the early 1990s, almost 400 recorded plant species had colonized the Spit (Higgins et al., 1992), and it had evolved into five distinct habitat types: meadows with a mix of grasses and wildflowers; forests, woodlands and thickets characterized by a mix of trees and shrubs; beaches, sand barrens and dunes formed by concrete slabs; wetlands; and aquatic habitats of submerged and floating vegetation. Among the over 400 plants and trees recorded by the mid-1990s were some nationally and provincially rare and unusual species such as prickly pear cactus (*Opuntia littoralis*), slender gerardia (*Agalinis tenuifolia*) and strange cinquefoil (*Potentilla paradoxa*), as well as orchids like nodding ladies' tresses (*Spiranthes cernua*) and bog twayblade (*Liparis loeselii*).

With flourishing ecological systems attracting the attention of urban nature lovers, the Leslie Street Spit's status as a civic attraction surged. Its appeal was also burnished by its status as a park underdog, an unexpected and unplanned greenspace that was outperforming any other parks in the region in terms of biodiversity and the density of the bird colonies. Ecological prominence may have been appealing to nature enthusiasts and people who enjoyed an alternative to the city's hustle and bustle, but the physical layout of the Spit also drew other groups, such as cyclists, who enjoyed the long continuous Spine Road devoid of cars. Photographers could capture stunning images of the city's skyline, as well as extraordinary combinations of natural features in a seemingly post-apocalyptic setting.

This new greenspace was thriving, in spite of the many dynamics working against it. For instance, its location within a heavily industrialized part of the urban waterfront would not typically be considered an ecological endowment nor could the fact that weekdays were dedicated to a continuous stream of heavy trucks dumping massive amounts of waste or the fact that it was a brand new landform

FIGURE 5.3   Leslie Street Spit fox kit, 2020

Source: Image by J. Foster

in what had previously been open water. But perhaps it was so successful precisely because the space had not been planned as an environmental feature and there was no overall vision constricting the range of possibilities at the outset of construction. Rather, decisions to protect and enhance ecological features were developed after nature had already taken its course. Probing the mélange of influences at play in the Spit's evolution, Sandilands (2017) observes that "what is interesting about the

FIGURE 5.4   Leslie Street Spit woodland meadow, 2021

Source: Image by J. Foster

Spit is that it appears to be a public *celebration* of ferality in a context in which most popular ecological discourse prefers distinction: wilderness versus city, indigenous versus exotic, natural versus artificial" (444).

Planning toxic urban ferality

For the most part, early environmental planning at the Leslie Street Spit was a game of catch-up with the habitat needs of exploding bird populations. Environmental plans came on the heels of fierce debates about the overall disposition of this extemporaneous greenspace. Relatively easy access to an expansive and unique landscape feature is a sure-fire recipe for a heated dispute. In the case of the Leslie Street Spit, competing proposals presented very incongruous visions for the future. The first round of landscape-oriented plans for the Spit was not, in fact, habitat-enhancing or even oriented towards improving the landform's ecological attributes. They were triggered by the Great Lakes Water Quality Agreement, which put an end to dumping directly into Lake Ontario in 1972. The City of Toronto had to come up with a legal and practical means to dispose of the accumulation of dredge that built up daily at the foot of the Don River. Habitat considerations were an afterthought. Perhaps unsurprisingly, the City also prioritized inexpensive options.

Spilling into Lake Ontario right at the Port Lands, only about 500 m from the baselands of the Leslie Street Spit, the mouth of the Don is engineered to form a hard 90-degree turn at the end of its channelized pathway through the city. Before the Don's combined groundwater and surface runoff enter the lake, water hits the hard wall of the Keating Channel dead on. This not only presents a major flooding challenge during wet weather events, but it is also engineered to fill up with silt and debris. As the base flow of water crashes into the Keating Channel, it accumulates and slows down. Debris and suspended particulates settle into dredgeate, which in turn causes flooding if not scooped and transported elsewhere. In order to remain functional as a river mouth (and avoid flooding major roadways, buildings and infrastructure), the City locked itself into a regime of daily removal of the dredgeate during the fall and spring wet weather seasons. The system of simply scooping it all up with a specially designed barge and transporting elsewhere worked fine, but only up to the point where it could be dumped into the easily accessible open water.

The hydraulic barge that collects and transports the dredgeate to the Leslie Street Spit carries 300 tons of muck per day through the fall, the equivalent of five full barges (Bateman, 2015). The average annual volume of the dredgeate removed from the Keating Channel between 2002 and 2007 is 30,646 cubic metres (TRCA et al., 2014). According to an environmental assessment of the lower Don River, the water in the Keating Channel is characterized by "elevated levels of conventional pollutants that exceed water quality guidelines even in dry weather or low flow conditions," such as bacteria, nutrient enrichment and contaminants, as well as extremely low levels of dissolved oxygen, high levels of suspended solids and elevated turbidity (TRCA et al., 2014). A study by the provincial Ministry of the Environment (2001) identifies a variety of contaminants in the dredgeate that include PCBs, organochlorides, PAHs and trace metals.

When the Metro Toronto Conservation Authority assumed control of the half of the Spit facing Toronto (the north side, along the city's inner harbour) in 1973, it was charged with developing a master plan for this new park that included regulations for visitor access. The rest of the Spit remained in the ownership of the provincial Ministry of Natural Resources, leased to the Toronto Port Authority. Over the next decade, dredgeate was deposited on the north side of the Spit, arranged to form a series of sandy peninsulas and embayments. This was a period of expansive landmass swelling, with approximately 6,500,000 cubic metres of dredged materials deposited between 1974 and 1983 (TRCA, 2016). These developed into a series of three cells that could contain the muck and isolate it from the lake, in accordance with the Great Lakes Water Quality Agreement. Meanwhile, in 1979, a new landform was created with construction waste on the lakeside of the Spit that was controlled by the Port Authority: an endikement that could protect the containment cells and the inner harbour. Future dumping was aimed at fortifying the existing landform along the lakeside and disposing dredgeate within the containment cells.

Conservation expectations heightened with the 1982 designation of the Spit as an ESA, due to its prominence as a bird magnet. As a result, the TRCA was

compelled to prepare environmentally sensitive plans to protect the habitat qualities that justified the status. Three portions of the Spit distinguish it in this respect,
and in combination they cover the entire landform. All satisfy the criteria of rare
species/rare communities, significant levels of diversity and significant ecological
functions. At the base of the Spit (42.7 hectares), the thicket, meadow, woodlands and wetlands host 28 vegetation communities and provide habitat for 2%
of Toronto's migrant songbird population. The spine and endikement extension
(63 hectares) provides 21% of the City's migrant songbird records, is an important
colonial breeding area and wintering area for waterfowl and provides snake hiber-
nacula as well as breeding habitat for toads and frogs. And Tommy Thompson Park
(191.3 hectares) sustains 31 vegetation communities, with 32 significant flora, 12
significant vegetation and 14 significant fauna species.

Debates raged over plans for the Spit through the 1980s, with very diverse visions
of what its ideal form would resemble and what functions it would serve. The
initial MTRCA proposal for an intensive aquatic-themed recreation district met
stiff opposition from a coalition of nature enthusiasts who objected to building a
hotel, amphitheatre, government docks, a private yacht club, 2,000 parking spaces,
a waterskiing school and camping facilities (Carley, 1998). That plan was modified
in 1987 to include only 565 moorings, some permanent parking, sailing clubs and a
public information and education centre (Taylor, 1987). Yet dispute about even the

FIGURE 5.5   Leslie Street Spit substrate, 2018

Source: Image by J. Foster

modified plan remained fierce, and the coalition of naturalists who preferred a non-interventionist "let it be" approach won the day after threatening to blockade the Spit. The coalition included groups such as the Friends of the Spit, the Sierra Club of Canada, the Federation of Ontario Naturalists, the University of Toronto Botany Conservation Group, the Toronto Cycling Committee and the Beaches Marathon Runners Association (Taylor, 1987). The coalition claimed to represent over one million people, and their strident opposition to the aquatic recreation park proposal generated dramatic headlines in the local media. They spurned any development, as well as any vehicle access beyond the dump trucks. Ultimately, the modified TRCA plan reached the final stages of approval in 1989 before it was officially rejected. From that point on, a hands-off approach took precedence and there were no more proposals for either development or vehicle access. Alongside the dumping activities, the Spit would become an urban wilderness refuge, managed with a light touch only for the sake of habitat enrichment. Within TRCA, the Spit falls under the administrative purview of the Restoration and Resource Management team, not the Parks and Planning team, and this resonates in design decisions affecting the habitat. The restoration team is populated by ecologists and biologists, and the unit's mandate is habitat quality, not public access or beautification.

Accidental ecology and the fallacy of letting it be

The "let it be" approach to managing the Spit has been very popular among Torontonians, and there have not been any significant challenges to this vision since the intensive aquatic pleasure park was finally squashed in 1989. Over the years, the characterization of the Spit as ecologically autonomous has become an enormously popular trope that few are willing to critically revisit. Many of the Spit's dedicated enthusiasts are fond of this portrayal because it is unique and signifies the power of nature and ecology to prevail in the face of destruction, to heal the scars of industrialization (Foster, 2007). For instance, it is described in the popular press as "the garbage dump turned accidental wilderness" (Forman, 2017), "North America's most remarkable public urban wilderness" (Ontario Trails, 2020) and "an unexpected urban oasis" (Otis, 2015). But the emphasis on the "hands off," spontaneous status of the Spit's flora and fauna elides the very "hands on" planning and management undertaken by TRCA that helps sustain its current biodiversity.

It has been a long time since the "let it be" approach was sincerely observed. The TRCA prepared the master plan for Tommy Thompson Park in 1992 and launched it in 1995. It incorporates the entire Spit, even though at the time it was prepared TRCA only controlled the half within the original footprint of Tommy Thompson Park (the side facing the harbour). The plan makes no pretense of letting the happy accident continue evolving without human mediation, but instead sets to guide successional processes with a strategy that is gradually implemented over time. The plan's intent is presented as "the adoption of the natural succession or ecological approach which relies on natural processes, augmented by minimal intervention and management of the park to achieve over time, the diversity of community types" (TRCA, 1992, p. x). Following the rationale of ecological protection that was victorious over intensive development attempts, the new plan seeks not only to safeguard existing landscape ecological features but also to enhance them by constructing new habitat. The plan identifies four key projects that create "seasonally flooded and protected pools for amphibian reproduction; mudflat areas for migrating shorebirds; flat open areas for nesting colonial waterbirds; shallow, vegetated channels for northern pike spawning; and sheltered thickets and den sites for overwintering reptiles, birds and mammals" (TRCA, 2000, p. 4).

In order to implement the plan, TRCA modified the Spit's ecology and topography in very significant ways. For instance, the confined disposal facilities were lined with clay to isolate contaminated dredgeate and a wetland ecosystem was graded, planted and furnished with sunken logs and other wetland habitat fixtures. In the intensive bird breeding areas, the eggs of ring-billed gulls and cormorants were oiled to control their populations. And sheltered backwaters were constructed between the peninsulas with berms, channels and a submerged gate to ensure access only for desirable fish. Of course, continual dumping, which includes not only the "clean fill" of construction debris but also the contaminated sediment trapped in the city's inner harbour, is the antithesis of "hands off." The master plan incorporates infrastructure for humans, such as construction of a visitors centre, public parking, a welcome centre and washroom facilities for environmental education, as well as an extensive trail system. The master plan also allows continuation of a sailing club with 100 swing moorings. Further, aligning the behaviours of the birding community with the *Tommy Thompson Park Owl Viewing and Reporting Policy* has been a chronic challenge. Most observe directives (such as staying at least 12 m away from birds, remaining in the bird's vicinity for only a few minutes, not baiting or using prey calls and abstaining from flash photography) and there is a great deal of care in the practices of the Tommy Thompson Bird Research Station and other bird research projects. But behaviours that threaten or endanger birds are not unusual at the Spit as visitors pursue a coveted photograph or identify a species off a bird checklist. All of these activities somehow have been overlooked in the romantic view of an ecosystem evolving without active management.

The first of three lagoons (also known as cells, or confined disposal facilities) within the Spit reached capacity in 1997, after which it was sealed from the lake, capped and rendered into the biodiverse habitat. This had been the largest of the three cells, and habitat was designed to create wetland conditions for fish and other riparian species. By introducing structural diversity both above and below water, as well as extensive planting to stabilize the shoreline, TRCA constructed a functional wetland that includes submerged amphibian shelter, snags for songbirds and nesting rafts for endangered Common terns (*Sterna hirundo*). TRCA characterizes this as "conservation by design" and commonly describes the approach as habitat restoration that employs "the purposeful act of designing for a variety of natural habitats while combining natural succession principles to create functional, productive areas" (TRCA, 2020). Complimentary work includes the enhancement of all of the embayments with shoreline planting and creation of "reproduction zones" and overwintering areas for fish and wildlife. Terrestrial habitat work incorporates new landform alterations for drainage and soil conditioning, as well as extensive planting. Other habitat creation projects on the Spit include seasonally flooded pools for amphibian reproduction, mudflats for migrating shorebirds, nesting areas for colonial waterbirds and sheltered thickets and dens for a variety of fauna. This is the only park in Toronto where dogs are not permitted since they disrupt wildlife, a rarity across Europe and North America. For the most part, this regulation is observed, especially after prominent signs were installed at the entrance explaining the rationale based on disruptive canine behaviours and stress to wildlife that perceive dogs as predators.

The Toronto Port Authority relinquished its portion of the Spit in 2019, and it is now entirely under the management of TRCA, as Tommy Thompson Park. In addition to the replenishment of the lake-facing side of the Spit with new debris, dredgeate dumping continues in the two remaining confined disposal cells. Although dumping to counteract erosion is potentially everlasting, dredgeate disposal will be less urgent with the pending revitalization of the Lower Don Lands and the Keating Channel, which is projected to be completed in 2024 (Waterfront Toronto, 2021). This massive project will introduce a floodplain and eliminate the Keating Channel's sharp 90-degree turn at the base of the Don River, hence attenuating the concentration of the dredgeate that is transported to the Spit daily.

FIGURE 5.6   Leslie Street Spit shoreline from the southern end, 2021

Source: Image by J. Foster

Clearly, the abundance of greenspace at the Leslie Street Spit has created spectacular habitat opportunities, and these are rightfully celebrated as unique features of Toronto. But the space is also rich in social opportunities – or rather, anti-social opportunities. For many people, it is the ideal space to find solitude, even seclusion. Because the Spit is relatively isolated while still being easily accessible from downtown, it is ideal for those who seek open-air solo experiences, without human companions. Finding space where introversion is commonplace and lone encounters with nature are feasible is not easy in a massive, dense metropolis like Toronto. For many visitors, it is a space that welcomes quiet contemplation, without having to undertake a strenuous journey or expose oneself to particularly dangerous surroundings. Unlike other large greenspaces in the region, it is not unusual to spot lone feminine-presenting people. And it is also popular with many people living on the margins of society. While the Port Lands have developed a reputation as a comparatively less safe part of the city, thanks to periodic news reports about assaults and testimonials from people who describe their own violent encounters, the Spit itself is not commonly known as dangerous terrain. Perhaps the absence of automobiles helps set the conditions for safety, since people cruising through in vehicles who might engage in physical altercations, such as police officers, cannot easily access anyone spending time beyond the entrance. Whatever the reason, over the years, the Spit has hosted numerous homesteads and shelters, typically tucked away out of sight from the main trail. It attracts not only people who fish recreationally but also many who do so for sustenance and nourishment, sometimes evidenced by small campfires near known fishing spots.

There are innumerable reasons people are drawn to the Spit, and many of these relate to the possibility of very low to no surveillance. While visitors may feel quite comfortable walking or cycling along the highly visible trails (particularly the paved roadways once used by dump trucks), they can also tuck away off trails between bushes, along the lake edges and into quiet areas. It is not surprising that the Spit is also known as a great spot to find queer companionship, especially among gay men. This harkens to Lupino-Smith's (2018) observations about queer occupancy and enjoyment of wild space that "some of the places where urban coyotes can thrive without detection and queer folks can hook up are the same. We share these spaces because they both need the wild within the city." The reasons for visiting are endless, as demonstrated by the preliminary findings of a project called Rubble to Refuge that seeks to understand human engagements with the Spit. Researchers have been impressed by the vast range of activities in which people participate, including pursuits like treasure hunting through the submerged dredge, composing poetry and musical scores, creating on-site art installations or foraging for meadow and forest foods. Clearly, the Leslie Street Spit is serving as an important alternative to conventional urban greenspace. In spite of its adjacency to the nation's financial epicentre and the labyrinth of high-rise towers covering the city's downtown and lakeshore, the so-called "hands off" approach has produced a landscape that defies social orthodoxies concerning how people interact with urban parks.

Greenspace as historical erasure

Nature on the Leslie Street Spit may offer delightful alternatives to the urban mainstream, but it is still part of a colonial project. By thinking about the Spit as an archive of the city's evolution, with materials relating to waves of development stored in the substrate, it is easy to track the rapid rate at which territory has been reconstituted over the past few hundred years. A far cry from the marshy ecosystems that once characterized the northern shores of Lake Ontario, the bricks, blocks, stones and concrete remnants are a testament to the progression of building techniques and technologies that have transformed the space into a city from the point of colonial encounter into the present. They are also a testament to dispossession and erasure. As a manifestation of the communities that were destroyed to make way for the high-rise towers, financial district and other incarnations of modernity, the materials at the Spit are the remains of people's histories, homes and livelihoods. In addition to Indigenous peoples, the project of city building invoked through the Spit displaced the low-income and working-class communities, dislocated in the name of slum clearance.

The legacy of local dispossession precedes the Spit, rooted in the erasure of Indigenous territorial inhabitation, landscape identities and livelihoods. Before it was an extension of the Port Lands, and before modern-day Toronto was settled as York, there was a long and rich history of Indigenous communities living on these lands. Indigenous occupancy of Toronto's shoreline stretches back at least to the last Ice Age, with approximately 65,000 Indigenous residents when European missionaries and traders began visiting in the 1600s (Bobiwash, 1997). In contrast to the geomorphological and topographical transformations by Europeans that drained and filled the extensive marshes, Indigenous people maintained productive relationships with these biozones, including inland riparian floodplains along the Don River, the swampy shorelines where the Don meets Lake Ontario, and the seasonally submerged freshwater lake ecosystems. Prior to colonial contact, the landscape reflected the intimate environmental interactions and land management practices of Indigenous communities. These practices continued well beyond the point of European contact, by communities of the Huron-Wendat, Seneca Haudenosaunee and Anishnabe/Mississauga. Jon Johnson (2013), a guide with First Story Toronto, characterizes Indigenous environmental stewardship as "mutual relationships of reciprocity and responsibility" and explains that "each of these groups, despite myriad colonial interventions and modern developments, has left an environmental legacy that is still evident in Toronto's landscape and in First Nations stories about places in this landscape" (61). Landscape artefacts that attest to this environmental legacy include sacred burial mounds, fishing weirs, black oak savannah remains and the city's oldest roadway (Davenport Road, a footpath used by Indigenous people for millennia).

In the region of the Leslie Street Spit, human settlement can be traced back 7,000 years along the Don River and Ashbridges Bay, evidenced by slate tools used by Indigenous people that were unearthed in 1886. There are also artefacts associated with Wendat longhouses villages established in 1300 (Evergreen, 2020). By 1700, the Haudenosaunee withdrew from the area and the Mississauga moved in. In the greatest act of deterritorialization in Toronto's history, in 1787, the Mississauga unwittingly surrendered over 250,000 acres of lands to the British for money, flints, household goods and rum. The sale, which amounted to approximately one dollar per acre, was believed by Mississauga to have been a rental agreement (Smith, 1987) and was revised with the *1805 Toronto Purchase*. It wasn't until 2010 that longstanding Indigenous legal claims that Canada had acquired Toronto unlawfully were resolved, whereby the Mississauga of the Credit received the largest land compensation in Canadian history (Mississauga of the Credit First Nation, 2020).

Urbanization was one of the key instruments of colonization in Canada, and the settlement of cities like Toronto presented an architectural opportunity to reconfigure the landscape according to European ideals and preferences. As resource-rich terrain that was occupied by Indigenous people, early colonial cities functioned as fortresses that expressed both extractive intent and dominion over existent communities. Expansion of these early cities "hardened" the colonial claim by fortifying the European presence and disciplining materials in service of the colonial empire (Foster & Schopf, 2017). The buildings that were produced through this process are almost entirely gone now, demolished and transported to dumps like the Leslie Street Spit, where their imprints are overlaid with vegetation. So too are the imprints of the pits and quarries dotted across southern Ontario, from whence the building minerals were extracted, which are also landscapes inhabited by Indigenous communities for millennia.

The urban Indigenous community in Toronto is very deeply marginalized. In 1997, the Indigenous population was estimated to be 60,000 residents (Bobiwash, 1997). The 2016 census data counting 46,315 Indigenous residents were rejected by the City of Toronto in favour of the estimated 70,000 residents recognized by agencies serving the community (City of Toronto, 2017). A 2017 study of the demographic characteristics of Toronto's Indigenous community reveals a poverty rate of 90% and a very low proportion (3.3%) of adults over 65 years (Rotondi et al., 2017). Meanwhile, in 2019, the Toronto Aboriginal Support Services Council reports that 63% of Indigenous adults in Toronto were unemployed (compared to 7% of adults in Ontario) and a rate of 35% homelessness (compared to 4% over the past four years for Canadian adults). Of those housed, one-third forsake key needs like food in order to meet shelter costs, and 26% live in dwellings requiring major repair. The legacy of discrimination against Indigenous people in Canada is well documented, including a 2015 report by the United Nations about the violation of human rights in Canada, the 2015 reports of the Truth and Reconciliation Commission of Canada and the 2019 report of the National Inquiry Into Missing and Murdered Indigenous Women and Girls.

The social determinants of health affecting Indigenous people in Toronto are deeply distressing. In addition to high poverty, homelessness and poor housing, a

2018 respondent-driven study called *Our Health Counts* reveals that 52% of Indigenous adults in Toronto have been incarcerated. An alarming 71% of this comprehensive study's respondents report that experiences of racism from health care professionals prevented, stopped or delayed them from returning to health services. There are high levels of food insecurity and elevated rates of chronic health problems like asthma, hepatitis C, cancer, liver disease, diabetes and high blood pressure. One-quarter of respondents have had a close friend or family member go missing, and one-third have had a close friend or family member die as a result of violence. The adverse living conditions of Indigenous people in Toronto are clear and troubling. Viewing these conditions in isolation from the long trajectory of discrimination and dispossession that has been sown and perpetuated through colonialism would be a grave error.

Toronto has always been inhabited by people without a fixed or permanent address, and until recently, the lower Don River and waterfront have been popular among homeless residents. In the century following the 1930s, the lower Don, which is the portion closest to the lake's rim, is described by Bonnell (2008) as "a repository for marginalized people." She explains that "for the individuals or families who found themselves there either by choice or by force, the valley seems to have operated as a kind of urban underworld, a place 'on the edges' that provided both refuge and invisibility" (2). Groups include squatters, Roma encampments, workers from the local brick factories and over 400 members of a "hobo jungle." It was also historically the vicinity of institutionalized "undesirables," with the House of Refuge (for poor, homeless and mentally ill Torontonians), the neighbouring Don Jail and two isolation hospitals that quarantined those inflicted with smallpox and diphtheria. It was a degraded environment where profuse waste was freely disposed of by residents and industries. With steep ravine walls and thick forest cover, the lower Don River proved less accessible to the police or other authorities and was attractive to those avoiding scrutiny. Informal homesteads and homeless encampments continued to flourish in the lower Don, along the waterfront and in the Port Lands until recently. Rediscovery and redevelopment of the Don mouth and Port Lands became a distinct civic preoccupation around the 2000s, accompanied by campaigns to remove the homeless community from these areas. This has, in turn, inspired some to quietly move to the Leslie Street Spit, where police have limited access and there are opportunities to shelter in peace, acquire food from the land and lake and pop into the city.

There are two destroyed communities in particular with specific material ties to the Leslie Street Spit. These are neighbourhoods that were demolished and disposed of as part of the city's modernist transformation. Linking archaeological excavation methods with archival research provides a rich understanding of the formation of the Spit. Schopf (2010) employed archaeological research and practice to document the material composition of dumping zones from 1964 and 1980, years that were notably active in terms of the disposal of construction material. The findings of her archaeological fieldwork develop an in-depth and detailed interpretation of the history of the rubble found at the Leslie Street Spit. Analysed alongside documents

FIGURE 5.7   Leslie Street Spit shoreline, lakeside, 2018

Source: Image by J. Foster

and records (such as old building reports, demolition records, brick catalogues, business correspondence, archival photographs, maps and indices), this multidisciplinary research enables the identification of the rubble's historical inhabitation at specific geographic points in the city and the surrounding landscape. Schopf's research presents a more refined understanding of exactly where and when and what was disposed. In follow-up work, Schopf and Foster (2014) investigate how the slum clearance and urban renewal projects of the 1960s yielded foundational materials for the Leslie Street Spit. This research contests the popular understanding of the Spit's composition and situates misrepresentation as a form of memory suppression and cultural erasure of marginalized people. Archaeological techniques offer unique insights in this case, since, as the authors note, "sometimes the only traces of displaced livelihoods are buried in dumps" (1087). But misrepresentation is not simply a matter of falsehoods contained in the city's official records and popular narratives. The celebration of greenspace is also enrolled in the practice of erasure, suppressing the unsavoury historical accounts about community destruction with pride in the ecological abundance that has sprung in an unlikely locale.

The stamps and imprints on the bricks at the Spit can be traced to local manufacturers, mostly pinpointed to what was once the countryside surrounding Toronto which is currently the city's outer and inner suburbs (Schopf, 2010). The escarpment and moraine that fringe the city provided expansive clay and aggregate materials, but these were also extracted within the city margins, for instance beside the brick factories of the lower Don River. The movement of building materials across the landscape illustrates the effects of the aggregate cycle on the southern Ontario landscape through time as it is recomposed and embodies the different lived experiences of diverse communities. Yet, the stories of specifically who inhabited these buildings and the communities within which they were situated are largely left unexplored. And the ability to trace minerals to specific excavation sites only tells us about the more durable buildings that constitute Toronto's built heritage, not those composed of wood or more perishable materials that were utilized by less wealthy, poor and impoverished residents.

The most obvious finding from this archaeological research is that the Spit was not founded on "clean fill." On the contrary, the contents of the Spit include whole households. Schopf found kitchenware, baby and children's effects, newspapers and even food items compacted in the 1964 stratigraphy. Indeed, quality control standards were not established until 1979, which meant that dumped materials were merely subjected to a passing visual and olfactory inspection (Ministry of the Environment, 1982, p. 4). However, these materials were of a particular character, comprising personal and household effects that were not removed prior to demolition. This portion of the Spit is now covered in vegetation, the roots of which are affixed to the remains of people's homes.

The developments that replaced the communities that are now located under the Spit's vegetation reveal a great deal about the city's ambitions, preferences and socio-cultural biases. Brick is a vernacular building material in this region, and Toronto's older buildings are easily distinguishable by their red and yellow coloration, consistent with local clay profiles. As detailed by Filion (1999), Toronto underwent a surge in modernist planning between the post-war period and through the 1960s. In downtown Toronto, this was typified by slum clearance and urban renewal. This meant that older brick buildings and downtown neighbourhoods were the targets of demolition (Lemon, 1985), consistent with planning trends that sought to develop orderly cities by razing allegedly messy and congested neighbourhoods in favour of segregated land uses, clean lines, prominent circulation routes (like elevated highways), blocks of public housing and dramatic skyscrapers with open plazas. Fillion notes that there was broad consensus in support of bold planning interventions and explains that

> Consistent with modernism's anti-traditionalism, planning visions of the period turned their back on the prewar urban form, depicted as ill-suited to prevailing preferences and needs because of traffic congestion, inadequate parking, deteriorating housing conditions and insufficient green space. The spread of slums was indeed an obsession of the time which sanctioned the call for extensive redevelopment and revitalization efforts.
>
> *(428)*

Concrete replaced brick as the desired material in Toronto, especially for new civic buildings, hospitals, universities, cultural institutions and city infrastructure. As a relatively inexpensive product that is imposing, malleable and durable, concrete became a staple of modernist planning. The mere possibility of concrete structures often foreclosed alternate planning possibilities, since audacious concrete structures were compulsory for any city with modernist aspirations. As summarized by Schopf and Foster (2014), the

> stories behind the rubble of the Leslie Street Spit demonstrate that the landscape of the Spit is much more than a nondescript mass of construction waste, but rather a landscape full of memory about the removal of undesirable built resources of the city and their replacement with new forms of architecture.
>
> *(1096)*

There are two specific neighbourhoods that are evident in the household materials of the Leslie Street Spit. These are Alexander Park and The Ward, both of which were primarily populated by poor and working-class residents living in modest homes. There are particular acts of demolition in each of these communities that can be linked to the personal and household effects buried at the Spit – for instance, teacups, bits of glass, medicine bottles, plates, diapers, skipping ropes, newspapers, electrical wire, rusted metal, eyeglasses, toothpaste tubes and food waste. Tracking insurance records, planning documents, building and demolition applications and media files reveals that these were the particular communities that correspond with the locations of materials deposited at the Spit in these specific years (Schopf, 2010).

In the case of Alexander Park, 200 houses were demolished on about 9 acres of land to make space for 380 units built in a modern building style (Sewell, 1993) and three towers. The demolished houses were constructed in the 19th century out of wood and brick. The lots and streets were narrow, and many structures were in disrepair (Schopf & Foster, 2014). Rather than reinvesting in the existing buildings and people in these communities, in 1964 the City expropriated 16 acres that eventually became the public housing complex. Toronto Community Housing Corporation is currently undertaking another round of demolition and revitalization at Alexander Park, which will preserve the three towers and introduce market condominiums, rowhouses, new retail units, private facilities and an open-access greenspace.

There is chronological symmetry between intensive dumping on the Spit and destruction of the Ward to create Toronto's new city hall and its public plaza in the 1960s. In this case, the city had already expropriated and demolished Toronto's original Chinatown neighbourhood in the 1950s. The arcades, low-end hotels and dwellings that were located at the site now occupied by New City Hall were razed in the mid-1960s. This was one of Toronto's most culturally significant communities, instrumental in the city's evolution into one of the world's most diverse metropolises. The Toronto Ward Museum (2020) characterizes the community as

> the first settlement destination for many newcomers to Toronto between the mid 19th and mid 20th centuries; home to Toronto's early Jewish community,

Toronto's first Little Italy and Toronto's first Chinatown. A densely populated and truly multicultural neighbourhood, it was also home to African-Canadians, Irish refugees, previously enslaved African-Americans and more.

Removal of these low-income communities is part of Toronto's history, a key point in the city's evolution as a metropolis replete with the aspirations and fixtures of modernism. The uneven impacts of creative destruction are indisputable. While the financial gains of redevelopment are certain, they are not experienced by all residents, and the cost of redevelopment is born by those living in the pathway of modernization in service of neoliberal economic globalization. Giving precedence to competitive capital markets escalates land prices and treats the types of neighbourhood spaces as commodities that can be reconfigured through cycles of expanding profit (Foster & Schopf, 2017). Gains for some are inextricably linked to the lost homes and diminished livelihoods of others, reinforcing social difference and reifying the power of capital by displacing lower- and working-class Torontonians. Masking the remains of these neighbourhoods as "accidental wilderness," however unplanned, is a strategic means of socio-cultural erasure and helps inscribe a delightful timbre to the material evidence of inequitable and damaging cycles of capital accumulation.

Marginality and opportunity in the city

Rubble is refuge at the Leslie Street Spit. But so are all the other forms of refuse, including the sludge dredged from the inner harbour and the household effects of lost communities. It is a place where unique and otherwise unavailable habitat exists in the midst of intensive urban development, on marginal land formed only within the past half-century. The spit is remarkable, not only for the ecological attributes but also as a space where social conventions are loosened in favour of more self-regulated relationships with the landscape. It is a refuge from the characteristic intensity, temperature, traffic and surveillance of the city. It is easy to understand why this landform is cherished and shielded from development.

Despite popular narratives, the Leslie Street Spit is not the product of a "hands off" approach, nor is it composed of so-called "clean fill." These are storylines that are tenacious yet demonstrably false. Hajer's (1997) conception of storylines as historically and culturally situated accounts that offer an explanatory framework for the evolution of environmental phenomena is useful in understanding the power of these narratives. Repetition of these storylines, to the point where they function discursively as unchecked received wisdom about the city's merits, also serves to efface the existence of Indigenous, homeless and historically marginalized people. The habitat is spectacular, and celebration of the ecological evolution of the space is certainly justifiable. But appreciation of the natural splendour does not have to ignore the less savoury attributes of the site through partial, incomplete or distorted interpretations of the Spit.

It is also easy to ignore vexing ecological questions at the Spit. One persistent issue is the ethics of creating contaminated and/or perilous habitat. In this instance, the protection tendered by the Spit enables ecological richness, but the landscape qualities are such that the health and wellbeing of resident fauna are potentially at risk. Why create habitat that attracts wildlife to harmful settings? What are the ecological achievements in producing contaminated or dangerous habitat? Two examples of species that are imperilled by the landscape circumstances at the Spit are coyote (*Canis latrans*) and herring gull (*Larus delawarensis*).

Coyotes on the Spit thrive with secluded dens, plentiful prey and vast range. They are opportunistic predators and scavengers that remain elusive. At the Spit, pairs breed and raise pups each year. Thanks to a network of connected corridors of greenspaces along the lakefront and ravines (an oft-cited regional urban sustainability attribute), they are also able to roam far afield. If they remain on the Spit, coyotes enjoy unparalleled habitat opportunities and all of their life cycle needs are fulfilled. But once a coyote leaves the Spit, it encounters severe risks. This has been the case, for instance, for those that have been hit by vehicles on roadways or shot by farmers in the agricultural milieu. As a top predator in urban settings with typical ranges between 3 and 15 square kilometres, the Spit is too small to support multiple sets of breeding coyotes on its own (Thompson, 2014). So they naturally take advantage of the adjacent greenspaces and the associated green matrix as part of their extended range. Predictably, coyotes from the Leslie Street Spit that were fitted with GPS radio-collars have been documented as roadkill (Foster, 2007; Thompson, 2014), and they are the subject of great fear among Torontonians who feel that dangerous animals are trespassing into human terrain. Conflict between those who feed and encourage coyotes and those who fear them inspired the city to develop the *Coyote Response Strategy* in 2013. The strategy focuses on education, a bylaw prohibiting feeding and protocols for removal, care and return upon recovery of injured and sick coyotes. This has helped settle discord, but it does not address the vulnerability of coyotes to road traffic as they make use of their interconnected urban range.

Research conducted by Environment Canada in 2000 identified high levels of the brominated diphenyl ether (Penta-BDE) at the Leslie Street Spit. In fact, this was the highest concentration in the Great Lakes, along with a portion of northern Lake Michigan (Norstrom et al., 2002). This is a bio-accumulating toxin that is prevalent in fire retardant products and affects hormone levels in the thyroid gland. It is banned in the European Union, due to reproductive and neurological risks, and was voluntarily phased out in Canada in 2006. The report finds that Herring gulls at the Spit are particularly vulnerable due to air and water emissions from neighbouring downtown Toronto and industrial areas, as well as historic contamination. The effect of this and other bans is evident in the 2011 *Toronto and Region Remedial Action Plan* report that finds the low reproductive success observed in Great Lakes herring gulls during the 1970s has been stabilized at the Leslie Street Spit. The factors currently affecting egg viability may include toxic substances as well as bacterial and viral pathogens (TRCA, 2011), suggesting that the constricted breeding area might be a consideration. A report by de Solla et al. (2016) monitoring contaminants in Herring gulls in the Great Lakes over the 40 years from 1974 to 2013 also illustrates the success of bans but finds that the Leslie Street Spit had the lowest overall decline among the fifteen monitored sites. The report explains the limitations of bans in Toronto by noting that

> the persistent nature of these compounds means that they continue to be available and accumulate in biota. Although PCB production was restricted in 1974 onward to use in closed systems only, prior use in open products such as caulking and sealants means that PCBs are still being released into the environment, thus maintaining their presence.
>
> *(176)*

The Leslie Street Spit provides a compelling illustration of several stages in the cycle of creative destruction that are underexplored. It lays bare the community dispossession, the end points of disposal and the craft of erasure through which creative destruction operates. The material effects and the socially uneven impacts of this prominent strategy for wealth accumulation are on full display. This "spatial fix" for absorbing surplus capital by replacing poor and working-class communities with grandiose emblems of modernism requires a dumping point. In this case, the unsavoury evidence of destruction is obscured through civic mythologies of "clean fill" and a "hands off" approach to the site's evolution. The inequities of these discourses are further obscured and deepened through the aesthetic appeal of accidental ecological splendour in the midst of a dense city. A verdant spectacle springing from ruins taps into a powerful aesthetic sensibility of the sublime, which can be experienced to full effect year-round at the Spit. It inspires celebration and devotion to these narratives but meanwhile elides the particular risks experienced by wildlife in urban post-industrial spaces, even on new landforms such as this one.

How do we plan for toxic ferality? And what is our responsibility to render history visible in vibrant greenspaces? Because they are spaces that are often in transition in terms of civic imaginations, post-industrial sites offer unique opportunities to elucidate storylines that are underrepresented, for instance, by making visible the colonial legacies that formed the city, as well as the histories and current existence of Indigenous communities in the urban landscape. We can similarly honour the communities that were destroyed by dispensing with myths like "clean fill" and acknowledging a more accurate composition of the Leslie Street Spit. These are essential elements of the storyline of the Leslie Street Spit that should become visible, alongside amplified awareness of the landform's role as a repository of toxicity. Meanwhile, we can attend to equity concerns in the present by ensuring that vulnerable communities, such as Indigenous and homeless Torontonians, remain welcome in these ecological gems. Minimizing surveillance, allowing informal homesteads and honouring landscape relationships that do not conform with mainstream appreciations of nature are essential to the legacy of the Leslie Street Spit as a space of unique socio-ecological opportunity.

Bibliography

Bateman, C. (2015, October 15). How Muck from the Keating Channel becomes new land for the leslie spit. *Toronto Life*. https://torontolife.com/city/don-river-dredging-leslie-street-spit/.

Bobiwash, A. R. (1997). The history of native people in Toronto, an overview. In F. Sanderson & H. Howard-Bobiwash (Eds.), *The meeting place: Aboriginal life in Toronto*. The Native Canadian Centre of Toronto.

Bonnell, J. (2008). Toronto's underworld: The Don River Valley as a 'repository for undesirables.' Presented at the Canadian Historical Association Annual Meeting.

Bonnel, J. (2009). *Don River Valley historical mapping project*. http://maps.library.utoronto.ca/dvhmp/ashbridges-bay.html.

Carley, J. (1998). The Leslie street spit. In G. Fairfield (Ed.), *Ashbridges' bay: An anthology of writings by those who knew and loved Ashbridge's bay* (pp. 105–116). Toronto Ornithological Club.

Carley, J. (2022). No other piece of land has attracted such passionate defenders. *Friends of the Spit*. https://friendsofthespit.ca/about-us/.

CH2M HILL Canada Ltd. (2016). *Community based risk assessment – Terms of reference, Port Lands, Toronto*. Author.

City of Toronto. (2017, August 18). *Indigenous people of Toronto* (City of Toronto Indigenous Affairs Office). Author. www.toronto.ca/city-government/accessibility-human-rights/indigenous-affairs-office/torontos-indigenous-peoples/.

Duric, D. The Toronto purchase treaty no. 13 (1805). *Mississaugas of the Credit First Nation* (blog). Retrieved June 9, 2020, from http://mncfn.ca/torontopurchase/.

Evergreen. (2020). *Indigenous beginnings of the Don River Velley*. https://donrivervalleypark.ca/about-the-park/history/.

Filion, P. (1999). Rupture or continuity? Modern and postmodern planning in Toronto. *International Journal of Urban and Regional Research*, *23*(3), 421–444.

Forman, G. (2017, February 14). Scenes from Toronto's Leslie Spit. *NOW Magazine*. https://nowtoronto.com/news/scenes-from-toronto-leslie-spit/.

Foster, J. (2007). Toronto's Leslie Street Spit: Aesthetics and the ecology of marginal land. *Environmental Philosophy*, *4*(1 & 2), 117–133.

Foster, J., & Anders Sandberg, L. (2004). Friends or foe? Invasive species and public greenspace in Toronto." *The Geographical Review*, *94*(2), 178–198.

Foster, J., & Fraser, G. S. (n.d.). Predators, prey and the dynamics of change at the Leslie Street Spit. In A. Sandberg, S. Bocking, & K. Cruikshank (Eds.), *Urban explorations: Environmental histories of the Toronto region*. Wilson Institute for Canadian History.

Foster, J., & Schopf, H. (2017). Urban ecological evolution through mineral migration: Extracting, recomposing, demolishing and recolonizing Toronto's landscape. *Landscript*, *5*, 47–64.

Hajer, M. A. (1997). *The politics of environmental discourse: Ecological modernization and the policy process*. Oxford University Press.

Harvey, D. (2001). *Spaces of capital: Towards a critical geography*. Routledge.

Higgins, V. J., Denzel, S., & Fazari, N. (1992). *Plant communities of the Leslie Street Spit: A beginner's guide*. Botany Conservation Group, Department of Botany, University of Toronto.

Johnson, J. (2013). The indigenous environmental history of Toronto, 'the meeting place.' In A. Sandberg, S. Bocking, & K. Cruikshank (Eds.), *Urban explorations: Environmental histories of the Toronto Region* (pp. 59–71). Wilson Institute for Canadian History.

Kipfer, S., and Keil, R. (2002). Toronto Inc? Planning the competitive city in the New Toronto. *Antipode: A Journal of Geography, 34*(2), 227–263.

Lamer, C. (2020, February 14). Accidental wilderness: The Leslie Street spit. *The Nature of Things.* Canadian Broadcasting Corporation. https://gem.cbc.ca/media/the-nature-of-things/s59e14.

Lemon, J. (1985). *Toronto since 1918: An illustrated history.* James Lorimer & Company.

Lupino-Smith, E. (2018, March 29). Morality cuts: Uncovering queer urban ecologies. *Guts.* http://gutsmagazine.ca/morality-cuts/.

Mainguy, S., & Kricsfalusy, V. (2012). *Environmentally significant areas (ESAs) in the City of Toronto.* Toronto City Planning.

Marche, S. (2010, May 17). The beauty of birding at the Leslie Street spit. *The Globe and Mail.* https://www.theglobeandmail.com/news/toronto/the-beauty-of-birding-at-the-leslie-street-spit/article1210693/.

Ministry of the Environment. (1982). *Lakefill quality study: Leslie Street Spit, City of Toronto.* Environment Canada.

Ministry of the Environment. (2001). *The influence of urban runoff on sediment quality and benthos in Toronto Harbour.* Author.

Mississaugas of the Credit First Nation. (2020, December 20). The Toronto purchase treaty no. 13 (1805). *Mississaugas of the Credit First Nation.* http://mncfn.ca/torontopurchase/.

National Inquiry into Missing and Murdered Indigenous Women and Girls. (2019). *Reclaiming power and place: The final report of the national inquiry into missing and murdered indigenous women and girls.* National Inquiry.

Norstrom, R. J., Simon, M., Moisey, J., & Wakeford, B. (2002). Geographical distribution (2000) and temporal trends (1981–2000) of brominated diphenyl ethers in Great Lakes Herring gull eggs. *Environmental Science and Technology, 36*(22), 4783–4789.

Ontario Trails Council. (2020). *Leslie Street Spit trail.* http://beta.ontariotrails.ca/trails/view/leslie-street-spit-trail/.

Otis, D. (2015, October 1). 10 photos that showcase Toronto's unexpected urban oasis. *The Toronto Star.* https://www.thestar.com/news/gta/2015/10/01/10-photos-that-showcase-torontos-unexpected-urban-oasis.html.

Our Health Counts. (2018). *Our health counts Toronto fact sheets – well living house.* www.welllivinghouse.com/resources/whl-publications-reports/our-health-counts-toronto-fact-sheets/.

Rotondi, M. A., O'Campo, P., O'Brien, K., Firestone, M., Wolfe, S. H., Bourgeois, C., & Smylie, J. K. (2017). Our health counts Toronto: Using respondent-driven sampling to unmask census undercounts of an urban indigenous population in Toronto, Canada. *BMJ Open, 7*(12).

Sandilands, C. (2017). Some 'F' words for the environmental humanities: Feralities, feminism, futurities. In *The Routledge companion to the environmental humanities* (pp. 443–451). Routledge.

Schopf, H. (2010). Development, destruction, domestication: Providing context for the rubble of the Leslie Street Spit. Master of Environmental Studies Thesis, York University.

Schopf, H., & Foster, J. (2014). Buried localities: Archaeological exploration of a dump and urban wilderness refuge. *Local Environment, 19*(10), 1086–1109.

Sewell, J. (1993). *The shape of the city: Toronto struggles with modern planning.* University of Toronto Press.

SLR Consulting Canada Ltd. (2009). *Subsurface investigation in support of the EA for the DMN and Port Lands flood protection project.* Author.

Smith, D. (1987). *Sacred feathers.* University of Toronto Press.

Solla, S. R. D, Chip Weseloh, D. V., Hughes, K. D., & Moore, D. J. (2016). Forty-year decline of organic contaminants in eggs of Herring Gulls (Larus Argentatus) from the Great Lakes, 1974 to 2013. *Waterbirds, 39,* 166–179.

Taylor, S. (1987, January 24). Metrobody approves $6 million Leslie Street Spit project. *Toronto Star,* p. A8.

Thompson, B. (2014). *Coyotes and their movement in relation to resources in Tommy Thompson Park.* York University.

Toronto and Region Conservation Authority. (1992). *Tommy Thompson Park master plan.* Toronto and Region Conservation Authority.

Toronto and Region Conservation Authority. (2000). *Tommy Thompson Park public urban wilderness: Habitat creation and enhancement projects: 1995–2000.* Author.

Toronto and Region Conservation Authority. (2016, January 22). About Tommy Thompson Park. *Tommy Thompson Park | Leslie Street Spit* (blog). https://tommythompsonpark. ca/about/.

Toronto and Region Conservation Authority. (2020). Natural area enhancement plan. *Tommy Thompson Park: Toronto's Urban Wilderness.* https://tommythompsonpark.ca/ natural-area-enhancement-plan/.

Toronto and Region Conservation Authority, City of Toronto, and Waterfront Toronto. (2014). Environmental assessment: Don mouth naturalization and port lands flood protection project.

Toronto and Region Remedial Action Plan. (2011). *Bird or animal deformities or reproductive problems.* Author.

Toronto Animal Services. (2013). *Coyote response strategy.* City of Toronto. www.toronto.ca/ community-people/animals-pets/wildlife-in-the-city/coyotes/.

Toronto Ward Museum. (2020). *The ward, Toronto.* https://wardmuseum.ca/blockbyblock/ archives/blockbyblock-2017/theward/.

Truth and Reconciliation Commission of Canada. (2015). *Truth and reconciliation commission reports.* National Centre for Truth and Reconciliation. https://nctr.ca/records/reports/.

Waterfront Toronto. (2021, November 19). The Port Lands: Project timeline. *The Port Lands – Waterfront Toronto.* http://portlandsto.ca/project-timeline/.

Williams, N. S. G., Schwartz, M. W., Vesk, P. A., McCarthy, M. A., Hahs, A. K., Clemants, S. E., Corlett, R. T., Duncan, R. P., Norton, B. A., Thompson, K. and M. J. McDonnell. A conceptual framework for predicting the effects of urban environments on floras. *Journal of Ecology, 97*(1), 4–9.

6

CONCLUSIONS

Post-industrial urban greenspaces present opportunities to challenge the norms of Western urban planning and design. As ruptures in the neoliberal urban fabric, they allow us to reconsider what constitutes a better future and how we might get there. In some ways, we are already there. When we see these spaces as part of our relationships with the world, not just as places in need of tidying and fixing, we get much closer to an urban sustainability that is grounded in aptitudes and potentials that could produce much higher quality habitat and better alternatives for people, especially those whose needs are not served by dominant mainstream urban experiences. Rather than converting these into curated parks and open spaces that attract wealthier residents and generate new capital (as frequently happens in old industrial complexes), we can think of these spaces beyond current conventional aesthetic codings of what is appropriate, healthy and beautiful. We can think about them in terms of how nature flourishes without human interference, how they can help to advance environmental justice and how aesthetic interpretations of our everyday environments can be channelled towards heightened ecological literacy and diverse expressions of beauty and care.

These greenspaces are figured by land uses that no longer exist, and they fit easily into the trend for re-discovering and adapting industrial ruins in ways that sanitize grit and distance them from the poor and working-class people with direct connections to their histories. In doing so, greening can obscure the political dimensions of ecological systems. These are biophysical spaces with specific histories, and their histories are enlisted in the cycles of urbanized capitalism that have shaped the Global North through the past few centuries. They are not just material and historical artefacts, but they are also about relationships with urban space, with one another, and with ecological systems. These spaces open opportunities to do things like move beyond heteronormativity, think about alternatives to racial capitalism or advance anti- and de-colonial landscape relationships. Beautifying

DOI: 10.4324/9781315106403-6

old industrial sites with artistic plantings or urbane lifestyle centres does nothing to address these urgencies and will almost assuredly deepen marginalizations. This would be a missed opportunity to confront historic urban environmental injustice, and it would be a missed opportunity to shift the momentum towards more just and sustainable futures that correspond with the needs and desires of those most affected by deindustrialization and its interconnected legacies.

These spaces are not voids, nor are they vacant. Real nature does not exist somewhere else, in a better form. Our factories are nature, our waste is nature and rail lines are nature. Although they may seem ugly and uninviting to many people, the ecosystems that evolve in the wake of industrial uses are valid, interesting and productive life-supporting environments. They produce fertile and abundant versions of nature that we might not recognize. They might surprise us, especially when we are conditioned to see degradation. The ways that nature self-organizes in these spaces are fascinating and confirm that any custodial relationships we may assume are misplaced. When we leave them alone, whether through neglect or decisions to suspend intensive management, successional processes ensure that life thrives in new and innovative ways. We have much to learn, especially if we receive Alexis Shotwell's (2016) invitation to accept that "Orienting ourselves toward flourishing, toward the contingent proliferation of ways of being we can not predict, towards surprise, opens us to the possibility that the world can go on" (203).

The political processes that produce post-industrial space are multi-dimensional. From a political economy perspective, they are part of a cycle of material and labour extraction that is embedded in globalization and the neoliberal strategies of late capitalism. They exist as an essential factor in the process of creative destruction (as mutable matter in the machinations of capitalism) and as a consequence of creative destruction (as the debris of capitalism in favour of reaccumulated wealth). Where spaces that once served capital accumulation become impediments to growth, they are jettisoned until they are replaced with new structures and instruments of growth. When open spaces of old industrial sites exist in a state of indeterminacy, as is customary, nature runs wild and they habitually become *terrain vague*. Paris' Petite Ceinture and Toronto's Leslie Street Spit remain largely *terrain vague*, and these are places where we find aesthetic, ecological and social contingencies and freedoms unavailable elsewhere in these cities. These places offer respite from formal design and surveillance. They are disorderly and constantly in transition. Their political standing, in many ways, is a counter-point to the institutional disciplining of urban space by the neoliberal growth machine. With its festering rot and deep contamination, it is difficult to romanticize Milwaukee's Menomonee Valley as *terrain vague*, but it is fascinating to see how community groups were able to mobilize the wildness of the landscape and preserve the community's blue-collar identity while advancing health, employment, education and quality of life.

What all of these cases have in common are land-based relationships in everyday spaces. These are not convergence points for tourists, nor are they the types of spaces that might have appeared in textbooks or course syllabi about ecology. They are the types of spaces that are commonplace across European and North American cities; perhaps so commonplace that their ecological attributes are regarded with sentiments ranging from apathy to neglect to contempt. Yet, they are the environments that saturate cities, and for many people, they offer the best wilderness experiences. These are spaces that are replete with the potential for meaningful connections with nature, and they are important spaces for affirming struggles for the right to the city. Detached from popular civic consumer preoccupations and the logic of urban development, these spaces present opportunities to live in and shape surroundings independent of state control, in ways that might be meaningful for people whose lives have been marginalized and unserved by the mainstream urban landscape. The local environment and the livelihoods of nearby residents, including those living right in the spaces, are foregrounded in each case.

Trajectories of movement towards environmental justice are different in the three cases examined in this book, and they each tell us something different about how ecology can serve as politics by other means. In Milwaukee, historically marginalized communities were struggling with poverty, and they were also cut off from the vast adjacent greenspaces. They were living in a toxic vicinity, with dwindling employment opportunities. This is a remarkable instance where strategies for post-industrial landscapes secured quality manufacturing jobs and created access to the river and surrounding greenspace, as well as other environmental amenities for local residents. At the same time, an Indigenous community with historic roots in the Valley advanced its own strategies for self-determination while independently supporting tribe members, blocking multi-national mining corporations in their territories further north and reclaiming their traditional lands. In Paris, environmental justice concerns focus on inequitable access to public investment in shared space and uneven commitments to safety and accessibility. In this instance, environmental justice focuses on not over-investing in the greenspaces of elite neighbourhoods and not reproducing conventional Western expectations about nature. It is about ensuring that unconventional, indeterminate versions of nature are also embraced, especially where these may offer survival pathways for marginalized residents. In this way, it is about allowing people to inhabit nature in manners that might foreclose access for elite and mainstream urbanites, for instance, when people need space to live or fulfil life needs. Environmental justice concerns relating to creation of and access to alternative urban spaces are echoed in Toronto, but the Leslie Street Spit also exposes how unsavoury and unjust histories can be buried beneath the greenery. The Leslie Street Spit demonstrates how easily people's communities and homes can become waste, and how easily their histories can be obscured by the appeal of nature's ability to heal and reconstitute itself amid the ruin. This is a warning about the power of greening to encrypt inequity through celebratory narratives, to inter the remains of communities standing in the way of neoliberal economic progress. It also tells us about the deterritorialization of Indigenous lands as part of creative destruction and the effect of this legacy on current Indigenous lives.

Urban political ecology can advance a critical understanding of how these spaces might become more equitable and sustainable by deepening the field's commitment to both aesthetics and urban ecologies, ideally in concert. Ecological systems in our everyday surroundings, especially in places where they might not be fully appreciated, offer some of the best opportunities for advancing environmental justice. These stories will always be incomplete, constantly in flux. They give us useful insight into the complex ways that ecology is always political, and how deindustrialization opens new possibilities for both environmental injustice and environmental justice. The cases of the Menomonee Valley, Petite Ceinture and Leslie Street Spit offer inroads into enhancing the field of urban political ecology, especially in response to the critical interpretation of spaces situated midway through the cycle of creative destruction, between disregard/rejection and rediscovery/investment. They help contextualize the specific qualities and biophysical nuances of ecological systems in urbanized environments, the patterns and functions of which are not interchangeable with non-urbanized environments, as political processes rooted in historic legacies of colonialism, racism, heteronormativity and other oppressive systems. This helps sharpen an understanding of how urban natures are politically cultivated as well as the types of nature that are desirable and possible in the present and future. In spite of the consistency and comprehensive scope of these oppressive systems, there are no universal formulas, procedures or blueprints for more equitable and just futures for post-industrial spaces. They demand site-specific strategies that reflect the needs and desires of local communities, particularly those that have born the most immediate brunt de-industrialization and those most severely marginalized by colonialism and urbanized capitalism.

The prospect of unlikely alliances and their power in building and establishing capacity for life in urban post-industrial space is a source of great hope, and it is a current that runs through this book. Writing about making "oddkin" through unexpected collaborations and combinations, Donna Haraway (2016) asserts that these are the conditions through which we become with and flourish, and they are not new: "Becoming-with, not becoming, is the name of the game . . . Natures, cultures, subjects, and objects do not preexist their intertwined worldlings" (12).

These spaces have been heavily modified, with dramatic physical changes to terrain contours, geomorphology, soil composition and hydrology. Climatic changes follow suit with altered temperatures, humidity levels and airflow. Given the mutation of these base conditions, historic references for biota are of little relevance to current ecosystems. Thankfully, these spaces attract flora and fauna that adapt resourcefully to the new conditions. While cities in general are composed of novel ecosystems, the particular conditions of post-industrial sites fundamentally defy classical interpretations of ecology. The combined forces of species invasion and rapid successional transformation produce ecological richness in such space, which is enhanced with unexpected alliances between species that would not typically mix in conditions they would probably not otherwise encounter. Rather than mistaking the establishment of weeds (as spontaneous volunteer plants are often esteemed) as evidence of ecological degradation, these might more fittingly be interpreted as faithful signals of ecological resiliency in cities. Matter, energy and life are constantly inflowing into cities. Seeds embedded in everything from the droppings of migrating animals to food products, imported commodities and the bilges of cargo ships develop into plants on inhospitable terrain, which in turn attracts new plants and animals and emergent habitat conditions. Nature is organized in new and interesting ways that are ecologically cogent in site-specific terms. When these spaces are left to be they might even become *terrain vague*, and they might attract unlikely alliances of people as well.

One of the most striking findings of this research is the unexpected combinations of people aligned in coalition towards more just and sustainable futures for these derelict spaces. In Milwaukee, the Menomonee Valley Partnership brought previously unfamiliar groups together, like the Forest County Potawatomi Native American Tribe and the SSCHC and the municipal sewage department. The impact of this alliance extends further, to fight the multinational mining extraction industry with a strategic partnership among tribal groups, recreation groups and environmental groups that had previously been in opposition with one another. This resonates with Hajer's (1997) conception of discourse coalitions as interactions between assemblies of similar storylines, lines of reasoning and framings of issues. Although participants in a discourse coalition may have different political and environmental commitments, they tend to agree on the plausibility of an explanation, interpretation of information and desirability of an outcome. Similarly, unlikely alliances emerged in Paris between ecologists and those advocating for the return of industrial freight carriage on the Petite Ceinture through support for self-sustaining nature on the tracks, in opposition to groups seeking gardening, agricultural and recreational opportunities. In this case, the desire to minimize interference and active management was stronger than other goals often associated with urban sustainability, like food production and formal public access to greenspace. In Toronto, the range of unlikely alliances is unlimited. The nuances of these coalitions are important, suggesting the deeper politics of efforts to green old industrial spaces.

The case studies in this book beg questions about the political and ethical allegiances of researchers. Being mindful of the ethics of care, healing and reparation that infuse the experiences and practices of environmental justice work is a starting point, and this includes work in opposition to racial capitalism, colonialism, heteronormativity and other systems of oppression. Researchers must be particularly mindful of taken-for-granted truths that buttress these systems, which might be expressed through seemingly innocuous thoughts and actions relating to things like beauty, safety and ecosystem health. Remaining alert to the power of "greening" to perpetuate and produce new inequities should be a priority. Because the ecosystems of post-industrial spaces are so easily derided, these spaces are particularly vulnerable to enrolment in conversions that serve capital accumulation strategies and reinscribe oppressive urban landscape relationships.

In addition to conceptual and analytical commitments, researchers must be attentive in their methods and relations. As noted repeatedly, the work must be approached on a case-by-case basis, where site-specific and community-specific realities inform theoretical interpretations. Again, this means giving prominence to the perspectives of those whose experiences are closest to the landscape and those most impacted by changes, especially community members experiencing vulnerabilities and marginalization. Max Liboiron (2021) asks, "How do we make afterlives and good land relations integral to dominant scientific practice?" (20), a question that could be put to any urban political ecology research. Not reproducing colonial and settler entitlements to Indigenous land, culture, knowledge and lifeworlds is a start, and Liboiron also urges rejection of universalized worlds, values and obligations. They point out that we cannot have obligation without specificity and that non-Indigenous researchers must learn methodological approaches that "stand with" Indigenous scholarship done by and for people within Indigenous communities. Leanne Simpson's (2017) promotion of grounded normativity, where "embedded processes as freedom" are pathways of decolonization and resurgence, includes clearer guidance for non-Indigenous scholars: get out of the way and let Indigenous people build nations on their own terms. Beyond respect for Indigenous self-determination, such counsel might be recalled in any setting where marginalized communities are struggling to shape their own spaces in the wake of industrial deterioration.

These stories of post-industrial urban greenspace demonstrate that there is not a single path towards an ideal or even predictable outcomes for nature in cities. Local circumstances and the specific histories, preferences and needs of communities are the necessary guideposts. These spaces will necessarily evolve in ways that are fully unexpected and diverge from the mainstream, and this is exactly what enriches the experiences of urban life.

Bibliography

Hajer, M. A. (1997). *The politics of environmental discourse: Ecological modernization and the policy process*. Oxford University Press.

Haraway, D. J. (2016). *Staying with the trouble: Making Kin in the Chthulucene*. Duke University Press.

Liboiron, M. (2021). *Pollution is colonialism*. Duke University Press.

Shotwell, A. (2016). *Against purity: Living ethically in compromised times*. The University of Minnesota Press.

Simpson, L. B. (2017). *As we have always done: Indigenous freedom through radical resistance*. The University of Minnesota Press.

INDEX

Note: Page numbers in *italics* indicate a figure on the corresponding page.

Printed in the United States
by Baker & Taylor Publisher Services